VLADIMIR CHERNOV

A Short Guide

Moscow Progress Publishers

В. Т. Чернов
Москва
Краткий путеводитель
На английском языке

Translated from the Russian by J. C. Butler
Editors of the Russian text
R. D. Bogoyavlensky and V. V. Ostroumov
Editor of the English text I. A. Romashkevich
Designed by M. M. Zanegin
Art editor V. K. Zavadovskaya
Maps by V. M. Sokolov
Layout by I. K. Derva

Ч $\frac{20904}{014(01)\text{-}80}$ 93-80   1905040100

CONTENTS

To the reader:

This guide is a short account of Moscow and its principal points of interest for the foreign tourist who is visiting the city for the first time and has a limited time at his or her disposal.

To describe a city as vast as Moscow is difficult, especially within a small compass; but we hope that this guide will help you spend your time in our city pleasantly and profitably and make a first acquaintance with its sights and places of interest, so that you will want to renew that acquaintance in the future. Several excursions have been suggested for a stay of three or four days, rather arbitrarily, we admit; but with our recommendations in mind you can plan your own sightseeing around the city.

Your suggestions for future editions of our guide, and comments on this one, will be welcome. We would be grateful if you would send them to the following address:

17, Zubovsky Boulevard, Moscow, G-21.

Please note the following indications used in the text:
 *—*interesting*, **worth seeing**
—*interesting*, **a must

Editorial work on the guide-book was completed on January 1, 1978.
Progress Publishers is not responsible for any possible subsequent changes.

SOME USEFUL HINTS FOR VISITING MOSCOW

HOW TO GET TO MOSCOW

Moscow, the capital of the USSR, is the terminus of ten railways, thirteen highways, numerous airlines, and of waterways from five seas (the White Sea, the Baltic, the Caspian, the Sea of Azov, and the Black Sea).

Through trains and coaches connect Moscow with the capitals and cities of 30 other countries. The foreign railway stations through which you may enter the USSR are as follows:

Skafferhulle (Norway), Vajnikkala (Finland), Kuźnica-Bialostocka, Medyka and Terespol (Poland), Viksani and Jassy (Romania), Čiernā nad Tisou (Czechoslovakia), Zahon (Hungary), Akkaya (Turkey), Julfa (Iran), Sukhe-Bator (Mongolia), and Manchuria (China).

Every day 3,700 local suburban and long-distance trains carrying two million passengers arrive at and leave Moscow's railway stations.

The Trans-Siberian Railway connects Moscow with the port of Nakhodka on the Pacific Ocean, and passes through the largest industrial centres of the Urals and of Western and Eastern Siberia. It is 9,436 kilometres long, and the journey from Khabarovsk to Moscow on the Rossia Express takes 150 hours, i.e., more than six days. The distance to Moscow from the Soviet Union's western frontiers, for exam-

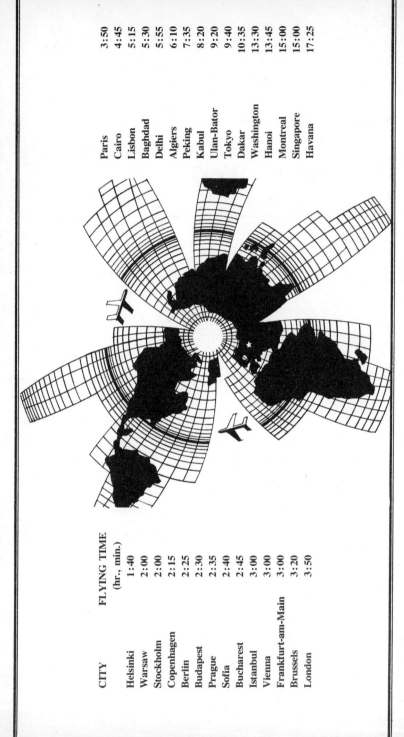

CITY	FLYING TIME (hr., min.)
Helsinki	1:40
Warsaw	2:00
Stockholm	2:00
Copenhagen	2:15
Berlin	2:25
Budapest	2:30
Prague	2:35
Sofia	2:40
Bucharest	2:45
Istanbul	3:00
Vienna	3:00
Frankfurt-am-Main	3:00
Brussels	3:20
London	3:50

Paris	3:50
Cairo	4:45
Lisbon	5:15
Baghdad	5:30
Delhi	5:55
Algiers	6:10
Peking	7:35
Kabul	8:20
Ulan-Bator	9:20
Tokyo	9:40
Dakar	10:35
Washington	13:30
Hanoi	13:45
Montreal	15:00
Singapore	15:00
Havana	17:25

ple, from Brest on the border with Poland, is 1,097 kilometres, and from Chop on the Czechoslovakian and Hungarian borders, 1,663 kilometres.

Soviet railways are noted for their high standard of equipment and excellent services.

However attractive the idea of travelling to Moscow by rail, road, or water, not everyone can do it, for some people just do not have the time. In that case they can turn to Aeroflot, the Soviet airline. Every day 450 aircraft on Aeroflot internal flights take off and land at Moscow's airports. The total length of Aeroflot's lines on internal flights is more than 600,000 kilometres, and on international flights 350,000 kilometres.

You can also fly to Moscow by other airlines. Aeroflot has joint arrangements with many of the world's major airlines, including those in the socialist countries, and lines like Air Canada, Air India, Alitalia, JAL, KLM, Lufthansa, Pan American, Sabena, SAS and others.

Air-passengers may book transit flights across the USSR without Soviet visas if their passports contain entry visas for their country of destination. Aeroflot passengers on transit through the Soviet Union may stop for up to three days in Moscow if they have tourist visas.

Today modern IL-62, TU-154, and TU-134 air liners are used on most of the international flights of Soviet civil aviation. These aircraft are noted for their speed, reliable construction, and comfort. The latest navigation systems ensure safe flight and landing in the most difficult weather conditions, which has all helped establish rapid, regular air services between Moscow and the world's biggest cities and capitals (see p. 6)

People who enjoy car holidays can drive to Moscow from or through Finland (903 kilometres from the Finno-Soviet border to Moscow), Poland (1,035 kilometres), Hungary and Czechoslovakia (2,035 kilometres), Romania (1,410 kilometres).

The Mozhaiskaya Motel with camping site and service station is situated on the Moscow Circular Road at the junction with the west-bound Minsk Highway.

Intourist, the Soviet travel agency (16 Marx Prospekt), arranges excursions for foreign tourists according to their tour programme.

In addition to Intourist, which caters for foreign tourists of every age group, there is the Sputnik Travel Bureau (15 Vorobyovskoye Highway, near Leninskiye Gory Metro station), which is primarily concerned with international tourism for young people.

Sputnik arranges numerous outings and excursions, Friendship Trains, meetings with Moscow's young people, and talks and discussions on various topics. It has its own network of well-situated, comfortable camps, hotels, and camping sites.

THE BEST TIME TO VISIT OUR CITY

That depends entirely on your tastes and interests. Many people prefer to come in summer, the normal holiday season, but it is even more interesting to visit Moscow in winter when its theatre and concert seasons are in full swing, and when Nature endows the city and its environs with special charm. There is nothing like seeing a real Russian winter for yourself. And the climate is not as severe as you might think. The normal winter temperature in Moscow is usually around −12°C to −15°C, and often even milder. Winds are moderate, the air is dry, and the rare severe frosts are therefore easy to stand. (Average winter temperatures in Moscow over many years are −7.8°C in December, −10.5°C in January, and −9.7°C in February.)

In summer Moscow as a rule is warm and sunny. The average summer temperature over many years is as follows: 16°C in June, 18.3°C in July, and 16.3°C in August.

Spring and autumn can also be pleasant times to visit Moscow. The mean monthly temperatures for these seasons are: March −4.7°C, April +4°C, May +11.7°C, and September +10.7°C.

The following table of weather lore may help the prospective visitor choose the best time to visit Moscow:

March 16	—snow begins to thaw;
April 12	—the ice breaks up in the Moskva River;
May 2	—Moscow has its first thunderstorm;
May 24	—the apples blossom;
August 26	—leaves begin to fall;
September 14	—the first night frosts;
October 28	—the first snow;
November 18	—the Moskva River freezes;
November 23	—snow cover becomes general.

Moscow is so vast, however, that the climatic conditions vary between centre and suburbs, and differ particularly in Moscow Region. The centre is drier and warmer. Outside the city it may be two or three degrees colder than in Moscow.

Generally speaking, the climate in and around Moscow is healthy and very pleasant for tourism.

WHAT TO BRING WITH YOU

First and foremost, of course, a valid passport and a Soviet visa, and return tickets.

What you bring with you depends, above all, on the time of year, on your tastes and habits, and on the length of your stay. But avoid bringing too much.

In winter it is advisable to bring warm underwear, winter boots with a warm insole, woollen socks or stockings, and warm gloves or mittens. It is also advisable to have a hat with ear-flaps. Women are advised to bring fur boots. And, of course, it is essential to have a warm winter coat. In summer a light raincoat will come in handy. From March to May and in September and October one should definitely bring a coat, waterproof and umbrella.

Chemist's shops and pharmacies always have a selection of Soviet and foreign medicines, but the tourist who suffers from a specific ailment is advised to bring the medicine prescribed by his or her doctor at home.

It remains to be said that a camera or cine-camera (8 mm or 16 mm) always come in handy.

MOSCOW TIME

Moscow time is two hours ahead of G.M.T. and operates in most of European USSR. Thus, when it is 12:00 in Moscow, it is 11:00 in Athens, Bucharest, Cairo, Helsinki, and Sofia; 10:00 in Belgrade, Berlin, Budapest, Paris, Prague, Rome, Stockholm, Vienna, and Warsaw; 9:00 in London; 4:00 in New York; 3:00 in Buenos Aires and Mexico City; 14:30 in Delhi; 18:00 in Tokyo; and 19:00 in Canberra.

Local time in Soviet cities depends on their time zone, and may differ considerably from Moscow time. Thus, when it is 12:00 in Moscow, it is 13:00 in Volgograd, 15:00 in Tashkent, 17:00 in Irkutsk, and 19:00 in Vladivostok.

THINGS YOU NEED TO KNOW

To make sure that you are met in the USSR (at airport, railway station or seaport) by representatives of Intourist, Sputnik, the All-Union Central Council of Trade Unions, or other inviting organisations, you should check before your departure that they have been notified of your expected time of arrival, route, the number of your air flight, train or name of ship. If that has been done you will definitely be met and helped with the border and customs formalities.

If it so happens that notification has not been received from your travel agency of firm, and you are not met, you should apply to any airport, railway or seaport official, or to a militiaman. All you need say is one word "Intourist". Intourist has agencies at all the international airports, main entry railway stations, and seaports of the USSR. The personnel there will take care of you and see that you and your luggage reach your hotel. Your luggage will be looked after until your departure.

Checking-out time at hotels is twelve noon.

The Soviet Union, like every other country, has certain currency and customs regulations for foreign visitors. Close observance of them will help you avoid undesirable misunderstandings and inconveniences that can arise when they are not known, or they have been misrepresented. You should, therefore, make yourself familiar with the main regulations, which are as follows.

The national currency of the USSR is the ruble. It is illegal to import, export, or send this currency in or out of the USSR in any way.

Foreign tourists may freely bring into the USSR foreign currency, travellers' cheques, letters of credit, etc., and precious metals (gold, silver, platinum and metals of the platinum group) as bars, items made of these, broken jewellery, or raw materials, with the exception of gold coins, precious stones, pearls, and articles made of them, but must declare them to the customs on arrival. A customs certificate will be issued to tourists for their declared imported currency, traveller's cheques, etc., which will ensure their unhindered departure from the country with all their imported valuables and enabled them to conduct transactions with them within the USSR.

In particular, foreign tourists may use the valuables they bring with them in the following way: change the foreign currency and travellers' cheques into rubles, open accounts in foreign currency, use them to buy goods at special (Beriozka) shops dealing in foreign currency, and also in Intourist bars and restaurants taking foreign currency.

Note: it is illegal to conduct any transactions in the USSR in foreign currencies, etc., except through an official exchange office.

Foreign currency and travellers' cheques may be exchanged for rubles at branches and exchange offices of the USSR Foreign Trade Bank and the USSR State Bank practically everywhere in the Soviet Union. Those currencies authorised for exchange by the USSR State Bank are accepted at the Bank's official rate of exchange which is published monthly in the Soviet press.

When foreign currency and travellers' cheques are exchanged for rubles on the basis of the customs certificate the tourist receives a bank receipt permitting him or her to re-exchange any rubles not spent for foreign currency on his or her departure at the border.

Tourists are allowed to bring objects and belongings intended for their own personal use into the USSR duty-free, i.e. footwear, clothes, underwear, camping equipment and sports gear, perfumes, cosmetics, and so on, needed for their stay in the USSR, according to the season. They may also bring with them duty-free (per person): one camera and one amateur cine-camera with the kit necessary for photographing and filming, one portable typewriter, and a reasonable number of small, inexpensive souvenirs.

Tourists coming to the USSR to hunt may bring their own hunting rifles with them, but they must have a voucher from Intourist or a foreign travel agency, confirming the purpose of their visit and that they are bringing a shotgun or hunting rifle with them. Hunting rifles brought into the USSR must be taken out of the country on departure.

The motor cars in which tourists drive to the USSR are allowed duty-free entry, on condition that they are used for the return journey.

Any objects may be taken out of the USSR (apart from prohibited items—see below) if they have been bought in shops with Soviet money obtained in exchange for foreign currency from the USSR Foreign Trade Bank or from branches of the USSR State Bank. The goods bought by foreign tourists for foreign currency in special shops and other commercial organisations in the USSR may be freely exported by them from the USSR if the receipts given to tourists by these organisations are kept.

It is prohibited to import or bring the following into the USSR: firearms, and cold steel of a military type; ammunition, gunpowder, and explosives; virulent toxic substances; opium, hashish, and other drugs, and appliances for using them; pornographic pictures and publications; books, films, gramophone records, manuscripts, etc., politically hostile to the Soviet Union.

It is prohibited to export or take the following from the USSR: firearms and cold steel; ammunition, gunpowder and explosives; virulent toxic substances; opium, hashish, and other drugs, and appliances for their use; and annulled securities. Antiques and objets d'art (paintings, sculptures, icons, carpets, furniture, fabrics, jewellery, manuscripts and books, etc.) may only be exported with special permission of the USSR Ministry of Culture on payment of a tax of 100 per cent of the value of the article, indicated in the export permit.

Before the customs inspection tourists are requested to fill in customs declaration forms, indicating all the articles made of gold, silver and platinum (including wedding rings), precious stones, pearls, etc. and the exact amount of currency and travellers' cheques brought into the USSR. These declaration forms must be kept until you pass through customs control on departure.

It is also a good idea to read Intourist's publication on customs and currency regulations, *A Reminder to the Tourist*, carefully.

If you bear these recommendations in mind, no difficulties should arise during your visit to the USSR.

A BRIEF SKETCH OF
THE CITY

Moscow is situated in the European part of the Soviet Union. The Moskva River, which flows through the city, is joined to the great Russian river Volga by the Moscow Canal. The city stretches 40 kilometres from north to south and 35 kilometres from east to west. Its area encircled by the Circular Road (109 kilometres) which is its boundary, is 879 square kilometres. In population (8,011,000) Moscow is the fourth largest city in the world.

Throughout history Moscow has played an outstanding role in the life of all the country. "Every Russian who looks at Moscow, feels she is his mother," the great Russian writer Lev Tolstoy said.

For more than 800 years Moscow has stood on seven hills on both banks of the Moskva River.

Many legends, songs, ballads and epics were created celebrating the beauty and grandeur of the main city of the Russian lands. One of them tells how Prince Yuri Dolgoruky ordered a wooden fort to be built and named it Moscow after the river on whose banks it rose. The first written mention of Moscow dates back to 1147, which marks the beginning of the city's chronicled history. Settlements, however, existed on its site long before that, as recent archaeological excavations have revealed, the most ancient being some 5,000 years old.

Since its very beginning Moscow has been inseparably linked with the fate of the Russian people; and it is not without reason that in olden times foreigners called the Russian state Muscovy and its inhabitants Muscovites.

Now let us glance at the map of the city. It resembles the cross-section of a log or tree stump, the rings of which tell us its age. The Kremlin[1] is at the centre of the city. Around it are five rings, historically marking where the city's boundaries were centuries ago, on which were erected wooden palisades, stone walls, and earthen ramparts. In the old days it was only possible to enter Moscow through special gates built in the fortifications.

The names of squares and streets still preserve echoes of the past: *Pokrovskiye Vorota* (the Gate of the Intercession), *Nikitskiye Vorota* (St. Nikita's Gate), *Petrovskiye Vorota* (Peter's Gate), *Zemlyanoi Val* (Earthen Rampart), *Valovaya Ulitsa* (Rampart Street), *Kitaisky Proyezd* (Kitai Passage, from the name of *Kitaigorod*), the area immediately outside the Kremlin, which formed the first ring[2] on the map). Today *Marx Prospekt*, *Staraya Ploshchad* (Old Square), *Novaya Ploshchad* (New Square), and *Ulitsa Razina* (Razin Street) are situated on the site of this ring. This central part of Moscow contains many historical and cultural monuments.

The second ring is known by Muscovites as *Bulvarnoye Koltso* (Boulevard Ring)[3]. In summer it is all green with foliage. For many years the city's suburbs began beyond its high rampart. The third ring is *Sadovoye Koltso* (Garden Ring).[4] Today it is a very important transport artery, running for nearly 16 kilometres right round the centre of the city. Further out we can trace the contours of a fourth ring,[5] once the Kamer-Kollezhsky Rampart, nearly 40 kilometres long, which some two centuries ago served as the city's customs boundary. A plan is being drawn up to turn this area into a circular road to relieve traffic in the city centre. Finally, there is the fifth ring built recently, the Moscow Circular Road,[6] which, as we have already noted, marks the city's present boundary.

From the centre a series of thoroughfares radiates out, cutting across these rings on all sides of the city. *Mir Prospekt* leads north to the Economic Exhibition and then becomes *Yaroslavl Highway*. *Leningrad Prospekt* stretches north-east to Sheremetyevo international airport. *Kalinin Prospekt*, which becomes *Kutuzov Prospekt* and then *Minsk Highway* runs west, while *Lenin Prospekt* leads south-west toward Vnukovo Airport. The two old streets, *Bolshaya Polyanka* and *Bolshaya Ordynka*, join, opening the road to the south, and *Volgograd Prospekt* and *Entuziastov Highway* lead to the east of the country.

Beyond the Moscow Circular Road stretch forests protected by the state, forming the city's Green Belt. In this woodland there are many

Diagram of how Moscow grew

recreation zones where Muscovites can spend their weekends. The Green Belt covers an area of 1,725 square kilometres.

Moscow has seen much and experienced much.

For nearly two and a half centuries the Russian people lived under Tatar-Mongolian yoke. Moscow played a leading role in unifying the Russian lands in a single state and in overthrowing the hateful oppressors in 1480.

The people rose more than once in defence of Moscow, which they saw as the heart of the Russian land. Thus, in 1612, the people's volunteers, led by Dmitry Pozharsky and Kozma Minin, liberated Moscow from the Polish invaders and their foreign mercenaries. In 1709 the Russian army blocked King Charles XII of Sweden's road to Moscow after defeating his troops at the Battle of Poltava. Moscow also played a vital role in the Patriotic War of 1812. At the Battle of Borodino, near Moscow, Napoleon's Grande Armée was dealt a blow from which it never recovered. Since then no invader has set foot in Moscow.

With the formation of the Russian centralised state at the end of the 15th century Moscow became the country's most important political, economic, and trade centre. Later it also became the focal point of Russian culture. There the chronicles were compiled and outstanding works of literature, painting and architecture created. It was here, in Moscow, too, that Russian printing began (1564), the first Russian higher educational institution, the Slavono-Graeco-Latin Academy, was founded (1687), and the first Russian newspaper published (1703).

In 1712 Peter the Great transferred the capital of Russia to St. Petersburg, which was built to his orders on the banks of the Neva; but Moscow remained, as before, the symbol of national, patriotic feelings of the people and the pride of the whole country. In 1755 the first Russian University was founded here. The work of the leading Russian writers and poets of the 18th century, Alexander Sumarokov, Denis Fonvizin, Nikolai Karamzin, and many others is bound up with Moscow. It was in Moscow that the great Russian 18th-century scientist, Mikhail Lomonosov, started on his scientific career. In later times many eminent writers and poets, scientists and artists, whose work greatly contributed to the development of not only Russian culture but of the world's, lived and worked in Moscow.

In the 19th century Moscow strengthened its reputation as the major centre of national culture.

Moscow occupied an outstanding place in the revolutionary liberation movement in Russia. Goaded by the excessive extortions and the heavy yoke of serfdom, the working people of Moscow more than once rose in arms against their oppressors in the Middle Ages for freedom and a better life. Major revolts by the city's poor and artisans flared up during the 16th-18th centuries (including the Copper Revolt and the Salt Revolt).

Moscow was closely linked with the Decembrist movement, the first Russian revolutionaries of the nobility who struggled against serfdom and autocracy between 1816 and 1825. Later Moscow University became a centre of the social movement in Russia; and it was there that the eminent revolutionary democrats Alexander Herzen, Nikolai Ogarev, and Vissarion Belinsky, began their activity. In those years numerous student circles sprang up in Moscow, supporting the ideas of the great Russian revolutionary democrats Chernyshevsky and Dobrolyubov.

In the 1870s and 1880s Moscow, together with St. Petersburg, became one of the most important centres of the working-class movement. After the emancipation of the serfs in 1861 Moscow rapidly became the biggest centre of industry in Russia after St. Petersburg, and the largest railway junction. The number of factories increased rapidly and the proletariat grew in numbers. At the beginning of the 1890s the first Marxist organisations in Moscow were formed; and in 1894 on Lenin's initiative the first city-wide Marxist organisation was set up. In 1898 the Moscow Committee of the Russian Social-Democratic Labour Party was elected immediately following the Party's first congress, the sponsors of which had included a number of Moscow Social-Democrats.

Moscow played a major role in the revolution of 1905-1907. The political strike of October 1905, sparked off by the revolutionary events in St. Petersburg (Bloody Sunday on January 9, 1905), developed into a powerful action of the proletariat of all Russia. In November 1905 a Soviet of Workers' Deputies was formed in Moscow, a mass organisation of the proletariat, and as the Soviet previously set up in Ivanovo, it was the forerunner of Soviet power. In December 1905 the Moscow workers, and first and foremost the workers of the Krasnaya Presnya district, turned the general political strike into an armed uprising which brought this first people's revolution of the imperialist era to a climax. In their struggle against tsarism the Moscow workers, led by the Party of Bolsheviks, displayed great courage and determination. The experience of the December armed uprising played an enormous part in the subsequent revolutionary struggle and victory of Russia's working class in October 1917.

In February 1917, when Russia was in the throes of the bourgeois-democratic revolution, Moscow's workers again actively responded to the Bolsheviks' appeal to struggle against tsarism, and the soldiers came over to their side. A Provisional Executive Committee of the city Soviet was elected on March 1.

In October 1917, on receiving the first reports of the victory of the socialist revolution in Petrograd, Moscow Bolsheviks set up a centre to direct the struggle for transfer of power to the Soviets. The bourgeois counter-revolutionaries launched an armed struggle against the revolutionary workers and soldiers; but after a week of battles, on the night of November 2, the latter, under the leadership of the Moscow Bolshevik organisation, crushed the counter-revolutionaries and established Soviet power in Moscow.

After the rout of the counter-revolutionaries the Moscow Soviet and Moscow Bolshevik organisation consolidated Soviet power, established revolutionary order and workers' control, and improved the living conditions of the city's workers. Together with the rest of the country Moscow took the road of socialist development.

On February 26, 1918, the Council of People's Commissars decided to transfer the capital of the young Soviet Republic from Petrograd (until 1914 St. Petersburg, and now Leningrad) to Moscow. This resolution was drafted by Lenin personally. On March 12 of the same year the red banner, the State flag of the Republic of Soviets, was raised above the Moscow Kremlin.

In December 1922 yet another historic event took place in the life of Moscow. At the First All-Union Congress of Soviets meeting in Moscow the Declaration and Treaty on the formation of the Union of Soviet Socialist Republics were approved and Moscow became the capital of the Soviet Union.

The significance of Moscow in the life of the USSR is very great. The capital is the seat of the Central Committee of the Communist Party of the Soviet Union, the Presidium of the USSR Supreme Soviet, and the Soviet Government. In it are concentrated the most important state and government institutions directing the life of a vast country with a population of more than 260 million.

Congresses of the Soviet Communist Party, sessions of the USSR Supreme Soviet, plenary meetings of the CPSU Central Committee, and various national and international conferences are held in Moscow. Here representatives from all the constituent Soviet Republics and of all the Soviet peoples solve the basic questions of economic development and work out the home and foreign policy of the Soviet state.

Moscow symbolises the unity and friendship of the peoples of the Soviet Union, and the strength and achievements of the socialist state. For every Soviet citizen Moscow and Motherland are synonyms.

Moscow is also the capital of the Russian Soviet Federative Socialist Republic, the largest of the fifteen republics forming the Soviet Union. It is therefore the seat of the RSFSR Supreme Soviet, and of the Republic's Government and other state and governmental institutions.

Moscow is a multinational city. Most of the people are Russians (more than six million) but Moscow is also inhabited by Ukrainians, Byelorussians, Jews, Tatars, Armenians, Georgians, Letts, and many other nationalities.

Muscovites are sociable, hospitable people. They love their city and are proud of it, and enjoy showing its sights to visitors.

Moscow is a major centre of international contacts and the meeting-place of many important international forums. Here, in the capital of the Soviet Union, which consistently stands for peace throughout the world and for international cooperation and friendship among nations, the envoys of different countries and continents discuss the most important questions of the struggle for peace, freedom, and social progress. At the end of 1973, for example, the World Congress of Peace Forces met in Moscow. No other international forum had been so representative. Around 3,200 delegates from 143 countries took part.

Moscow long ago became the symbol of peace and friendship among nations for millions of people all over the world. As far back as 1951 the Supreme Soviet of the USSR met in Moscow to pass a law on the defence of peace stipulating that any form of war propaganda is the gravest of crimes against humanity. In 1971 the Peace Programme adopted by the 24th Congress of the CPSU was broadcast from Moscow to the whole world, and since then it has been consistently implemented by the Soviet Government. It was here in Moscow that the Communist Party adopted its historic Programme approved and supported by the whole Soviet people, a programme which states: "Communism accomplishes the historic mission of delivering all men from social inequality, from every form of oppression and exploitation, from the horrors of war, and proclaims *Peace, Labour,*

Freedom, Equality, Fraternity and Happiness for all peoples of the earth."

On October 7, 1977, shortly before the sixtieth anniversary of the Great October Socialist Revolution, the Supreme Soviet of the USSR, expressing the will of the Soviet people, endorsed the new Constitution of the Union of Soviet Socialist Republics—the Fundamental Law of the developed socialist society. The new Constitution stipulates that "in the USSR war propaganda is banned".

Moscow is always happy to see visitors desiring lasting peace and international cooperation and closer economic and cultural relations. The number of foreign tourists increases with every year. In 1977 there were 4.4 million, and most of them, of course, visited Moscow.

Every year various international congresses, symposiums, and exhibitions are held here. The Moscow International Film Festival, the Tchaikovsky International Music Competition, the Moscow Stars (May 5-13), and the Russian Winter (December 25-January 5) festivals of Soviet art have become established events enjoying great prestige abroad.

Before World War II Moscow became the main political, economic, and cultural centre of the Soviet Union. Big factories, research centres, and educational establishments were built here, and the reconstruction of the city was started on a vast scale. It was being transformed before one's very eyes.

In the summer of 1941 the peaceful work of all Soviet people was disrupted: on June 22, without declaration of war nazi Germany treacherously attacked the Soviet Union. The Great Patriotic War against nazism began. Moscow suffered severe trials. The nazis resolved to seize the Soviet capital in the shortest possible time. Around 80 German divisions, including 14 armoured and 8 motorised divisions, attacked the city. The enemy threw hundreds of aircraft, thousands of tanks, guns, and mortars into action. Hitler declared he would inspect his troops in person at a victory parade in Moscow.

This, however, was never held. Another parade took place. On November 7, 1941 the 24th anniversary of the Great October Socialist Revolution, Soviet troops marched sternly through Red Square and went straight to the frontlines. A great battle was fought near Moscow. These were really trying days—the front was then on the very approaches to the capital, but all the Soviet people rose in Moscow's defence, for the outcome of the war and the nation's destiny were at stake. The troops of the Soviet Army and the citizens of the capital displayed unprecedented heroism and selflessness in the battles. More than 500,000 Muscovites built defence works and 168,000 applied to join the ranks of the People's Volunteers. People of Moscow and the Moscow Region operated valiantly in the rear of Hitler's troops. The nazi air force made more than 12,000 sorties on Moscow without achieving success; during the whole war only around 200 aircraft penetrated to the capital.

"Russia is vast, but there's nowhere to retreat, Moscow's behind us." All the city's defenders heard these words of the defence hero Vassily Klochkov, who hurled himself with a grenade beneath an enemy tank. They displayed the greatest valour and mass heroism and did not waver before the enemy. In December 1941 Soviet troops went over to the offensive and threw the enemy back from Moscow. So, at the walls of Moscow the nazi troops suffered their first major defeat of World War II. It was here that the myth of the invincibility of Hitler's army was dispelled.

For the outstanding services to the country, heroism and fortitude displayed by the people of the city, Moscow was awarded the honorary title of Hero City and decorated with the highest Soviet award, the Order of Lenin and the Gold Star medal. Over a million people were decorated with the Defence of Moscow medal, and the title of Hero of the Soviet Union was conferred on more than 800 Muscovites for their battle feats during the Great Patriotic War.

Moscow's postwar development has been the most dynamic in its history. The city has become the most important industrial centre of the country. Before the Revolution it was referred to as a "cotton town" (38 per cent of its workers were employed in the textile industry and only 18 per cent in the metal-working industries). Just before the war it became a "metal city".

Today the engineering and instrument-making industries are the leading branches here. Moscow produces motor vehicles, automatic transfer lines, machine tools, bearings, electrical engineering equipment, radio apparatus, electronic devices, and computers. At the same time it remains a major centre of light industry. The total volume of production is 211 times what it was before the Revolution, and is growing and improving with every year. The city's industrial development continues, mainly through the reconstruction and technical re-equipment of the existing enterprises, growth of labour productivity, and the formation of major industrial firms, combines, and amalgamations.

All Muscovites, like all the country's adult population, have work. There has been no unemployment since 1930. Thirty-eight per cent of all its workers are employed in industry and building, 30 per cent in science, education, the health service, and the arts, 8 per cent in transport, 5 per cent in housing and communal services, and 10 per cent in service industries, trade, and public catering; 5 per cent of all the industrial, office, and professional workers are employed in the government, economic, and banking apparatus.

Moscow is the main scientific centre of the Soviet Union. The USSR Academy of Sciences, the national academies of medical, agricultural and pedagogical sciences, the USSR Academy of Arts, and other specialised academies, and a large number of research institutes are located here. Nearly 300,000 scientists and researchers work in Moscow, many of them world famous. The city has 76 higher educational establishments with an enrollment of over 635,000 students. More than 18,000 graduates are studying in post-graduate departments. Specialists of the most varied professions with diplomas from Moscow's universities and colleges work in many towns and villages of the Soviet Union, and in many countries abroad. The Lomonosov Moscow State University is the main institution of higher learning in Moscow and the whole country (see pp. 133-134).

In 1960 the Patrice Lumumba Peoples' Friendship University was founded in Moscow. More than 3,000 of the 4,500 students and post-graduates in its six departments come from nearly 90 countries. The University trains highly qualified engineers, doctors, agronomists, lawyers, economists, teachers, etc., educated in the spirit of friendship among nations, for the developing countries of Asia, Africa, and Latin America.

Over the centuries Moscow has become one of the biggest cultural centres and one of the most beautiful cities in the world, and is rich in splendid monuments of Russian architecture. The fame of the monumental cathedrals and towers of the Moscow Kremlin, St. Basil's Cathedral (the Cathedral of the Intercession) on Red Square, the Novodevichy Convent and the Andronikov Monastery, the old Moscow churches, and unique civil architecture, has spread throughout the world. Not to mention the cosy, inimitable little side-streets off Arbat. When you walk down these you feel you have been carried many decades back in time.

Visitors to Moscow, no matter how little time they have available, naturally do not want to miss the pleasure of seeing these works of Russian architects that have now become national treasures.

Moscow's museums and picture galleries house collections of the works of brilliant old Russian and foreign masters and outstanding contemporary artists. The city has more than sixty museums: history of the revolution, historical, art, scientific and technical, literary, and theatrical museums (see pp. 161-162), visited by more than 17 million people a year.

Moscow has 32 theatres with permanent companies and large repertoires, 13 concert halls, two circuses, several film studios. Muscovites are great film-goers; the city has 120 cinemas most of which were built after World War II, and a total of 536 halls where films are shown, since nearly all the 400 workers' clubs and Palaces of Culture have auditoriums fitted with film projectors. Amateur art activities are highly developed, more than 200,000 Muscovites taking part in various circles, drama classes, studios, etc. The city has a number of amateur theatres in which, in the evening after work, factory and office workers, students, and old age pensioners, all united by love of art, take the boards.

Moscow has more than 4,500 libraries with over 300 million copies of books, newspapers, magazines, and other publications (before the Revolution the city had only twelve public libraries). A total of 18,500 million copies of newspapers, and 2,000 million copies of magazines and journals are published in Moscow annually. *Pravda*, the country's most widely read newspaper, has a daily print of nearly 11 million copies. Every day Muscovites receive over nine million copies of newspapers and magazines to which they have subscribed in advance, and around four million more are sold at newspaper kiosks.

The city has 2,400 monuments, buildings and other structures of historical and cultural value, all of them under state protection. Muscovites especially cherish everything connected with the memory of Lenin. In the city itself and in the Moscow Region there are more than 150 factories, institutions, houses, and flats which Lenin visited, spoke at, or worked in at various times. Memorial plaques have been placed on them. Lenin's name was given to one of Moscow's most beautiful avenues, to the Moscow

Metro, the USSR's biggest public library, the central stadium and to many of the foremost enterprises, scientific organisations, and educational establishments.

Soviet people are proud of their social achievements.

There are no privileged classes in the USSR, but there is a saying, "Children are the only privileged class in our country". The state and society surround them with care right from the cradle.

Old Muscovites recall that before the Revolution there were no kindergartens or creches in Moscow. Today almost everyone wishing to, can put his child in a creche or a kindergarten at a very low cost. Eighty per cent of the money spent on pre-school institutions for children comes from state appropriations and only 20 per cent is borne by the parents. Every year about 600,000 Moscow schoolchildren spend their summer holidays at Pioneer camps in picturesque spots around Moscow.

There are over 1,200 schools, attended by nearly 900,000 boys and girls. Another 90,000 young factory and office workers go to evening classes. Moscow has had universal literacy for a long time. Every third person in the city in the 20 to 29 age group has either complete or incomplete higher education, or specialised secondary education; and the transition is now being completed both in the capital and throughout the country to universal compulsory secondary education, either in a ten-year general school or in vocational and other specialised secondary schools. Moscow has around 300 vocational and technical schools and colleges where more than 300,000 young people are mastering the most diverse occupations.

All Soviet people receive free qualified medical treatment from a non-contributory health service. This means that treatment in clinics and hospitals, including the medicine administered in hospitals, is gratis. For the working days he has missed every sick worker receives up to 100 per cent of his average earnings. All medical institutions are financed by the state. Appropriations to extend Moscow's health service increase year by year, and now account for nearly a quarter of the city's budget. The city has 66,000 doctors and 117,000 qualified paramedical personnel, and over 260 hospitals with 115,000 beds. Preventive treatment is now the principal measure to protect citizens' health, and for that purpose large-scale medical check ups are carried out each year. The average life span in the city is now twice what it was before the Revolution.

Sport helps to improve health, and is now very popular in the Soviet Union. There are thousands of sports grounds, gyms, swimming pools, and stadiums in Moscow.

In 800-odd years the appearance of Moscow has changed many times, but the most striking changes have taken place since the Great October Socialist Revolution, and especially since World War. II. The city boundaries have been extended (its area is now five times what it was in 1917), it has soared upward, and has become brighter and more beautiful.

In his day Lenin stressed the need to reconstruct the vast city. In 1935 the first scientifically based general plan for its reconstruction was approved and work began on a broad scale.

After the war the Soviet Government adopted a new ten-year plan of Moscow's reconstruction for 1951-60, which was fully implemented.

The 24th Congress of the CPSU, held in 1971, posed the task of making the capital of the USSR a model Communist city, an idea which Lenin advanced in the 1920s. Muscovites and the whole Soviet people enthusiastically welcomed the decision. A new general plan for the next 25 to 30 years was drawn up and is now being implemented. It envisages the comprehensive solution of a wide range of town-building problems. Its main aim is to transform Moscow into a city with a convenient layout and modern architecture, and a high standard of public amenities. In particular, the plan envisages improvement of the traditional radial-concentric pattern that has grown up over the ages. The plan determines in practical terms how the city will look on the threshold of the third millennium. While preserving its distinctive features, Moscow will become even more beautiful and modern, reflecting in its appearance the lofty concepts of the age of socialism and communism.

Moscow is building, which explains why there are so many lorries and trucks on the streets with building materials, large prefabricated panels for housing, steel girders and reinforcing, and ferro-concrete structural elements. Every year on average 112,000 new flats with all modern conveniences are built. And as everywhere in the Soviet Union, Muscovites get most of these flats free without key money or down payments, and pay a very low monthly rental that includes running hot and cold water and central heating (the total rental works out at around 3 per cent of the average family budget).

One can say that Moscow has been redeveloped; four-fifths of its housing has been built since World War II. Whole new residential areas have appeared on the city map. Where there were little villages and waste-land broad, light avenues have been built, like Lenin Prospekt, Komsomol Prospekt, Kutuzov Prospekt, and Vernadsky Prospekt. New architectural ensembles and complexes have come into being, e.g. the Kremlin Palace of Congresses, the Young Pioneers' Palace on the Lenin Hills, the Lenin Central Stadium at Luzhniki, the Borodino Panorama on Kutuzov Prospekt, the Rossia and Intourist hotels, the headquarters of the Council for Mutual Economic Assistance, the Council of Ministers of the Russian Federation, the Television Centre and huge TV-tower at Ostankino, the Rossia and Oktyabr cinemas, the Moskva Swimming Pool, the residential and office buildings and shops on Kalinin Prospekt, the new Circus on Vernadsky Prospekt, and many sports facilities for the 1980 Olympics.

That completes our brief sketch of Moscow. Now let us take a walk along its streets and squares, proceeding leisurely so that we can take a good look at the city. That way you will learn many interesting things about our Soviet capital, whose heart-beat has always been at one with the rest of the country.

SOME DATES FROM MOSCOW'S HISTORY

Historic period or year	Event
1147	Moscow is first mentioned in the chronicles
1156	The Kremlin's first wooden walls and fortifications are built
1238	Moscow is sacked and burned by the Tatar hordes of Batu Khan

Historic period or year	Event
1367	The first stone walls of the Kremlin are laid
1480	The two-and-a-half century Tatar-Mongolian yoke is broken
1485-95	The present brick walls and towers of the Kremlin are built
End of the 15th century	The centralised Russian State is formed with Moscow as its seat
1555-61	St. Basil's Cathedral (the Cathedral of the Intercession) is built
1612	Moscow is liberated from Polish interventionists by the people's voluntary levies led by Kozma Minin and Dmitry Pozharsky
1633	The city's first rising main is laid
1655	The first cotton mill is built in the city
1687	The Slavono-Graeco-Latin Academy, the first higher educational institution in Russia is founded
1700	Cobblestone paving is laid on Moscow streets
1703	The first Russian newspaper, *Vedomosti*, is published
1712	On Peter the Great's edict the capital of Russia is transferred to St. Petersburg
1755	The first Russian University is founded in Moscow
1812	Napoleon's troops flee. The Russian people achieve victory in the Patriotic War
1816-25	The Decembrists, the first revolutionaries of the Russian nobility, are active in Moscow
1824	The Maly Theatre is founded
1825	The Bolshoi Theatre is founded

Historic period or year	Event
1851	The first train runs on the St. Petersburg-Moscow line
1861	Serfdom is abolished
1872	Russia's first higher educational institution for women is founded
1894	The Central Workers' Circle is formed, marking the beginning of the Moscow City Social-Democratic organisation
1895	For the first time Moscow workers hold public rallies to celebrate May Day, the day of international workers' solidarity
1895	The first Moscow trams run
1898	The Moscow Committee of the Russian Social-Democratic Labour Party is formed
1898	The Moscow Art Theatre is founded
1905-07	The first bourgeois-democratic revolution in Russia, the first people's revolution in the era of imperialism
1905	The October political strike. The December armed uprising of Moscow workers
November 1905	The Moscow Soviet of Workers' Deputies (a council of elected representatives from the city's factories and a prototype of Soviet power) is formed
February 1917	The February bourgeois-democratic revolution in Russia. The tsarist autocracy is overthrown
November 1917	The socialist revolution is accomplished. Soviet power is proclaimed in Moscow
March 12, 1918	Moscow becomes the capital of Soviet Russia
July 1918	The Constitution of the RSFSR, the first Soviet constitution, is adopted by the 5th All-Russia Congress of Soviets

Historic period or year	Event
April 1919	The first communist *subbotniks* are organised by Moscow workers
December 1920	The 8th All-Russia Congress of Soviets approves GOELRO, the plan for the electrification of Russia drawn up on Lenin's instructions
December 1922	The First All-Union Congress of Soviets in Moscow adopts the Declaration on the formation of the Union of Soviet Socialist Republics. Moscow becomes the capital of the USSR
October 19, 1923	Lenin visits Moscow for the last time
January 21, 1924	Lenin dies
1924	The first Soviet motor car is produced in Moscow
1925	The 14th Congress of the CPSU(B) meets in Moscow and adopts the policy of socialist industrialisation
1927	The 15th Congress of the CPSU(B) adopts the policy of collectivisation of agriculture
1931	The AMO Motor Works is commissioned
1935	The first Metro line is commissioned
1935	The first plan for the reconstruction of Moscow is adopted
1936	The Constitution of the USSR is adopted by the 8th All-Union Congress of Soviets
1937	The Crews of Valery Chkalov and Mikhail Gromov accomplish the first non-stop flights of Soviet aircraft from Moscow to the USA across the North Pole
1937	The Moscow Canal, joining the Moskva and the Oka rivers with the Volga, is commissioned
June 22, 1941	Nazi Germany attacks the Soviet Union

Historic period or year	Event
December 6, 1941	The rout of nazi troops begins near Moscow
August 5, 1943	The first triumphant artillery salute of the war is fired to celebrate the liberation of Orel and Belgorod from nazi invaders. Similar salutes on the occasion of the Soviet Army's victories later become traditional
May 8, 1945	Nazi Germany surrenders. The Soviet people's Great Patriotic War against German fascist invaders ends victoriously
June 24, 1945	The Victory Parade is held in Moscow
September 1947	Moscow celebrates its 800th anniversary
1951	The second general plan for the reconstruction of Moscow is adopted
1951-53	Moscow's first skyscrapers are erected
1953	The new building of Moscow University is commissioned on the Lenin Hills
September 1956	The TU-104 turbo-jet passenger aircraft accomplishes its first flight
1956	The Lenin Central Stadium built
1957	The 6th World Festival of Youth and Students is held in Moscow
November 1957, November 1960, June 1969	Representatives of communist and workers' parties hold an International Meeting in Moscow
1960	The Patrice Lumumba Peoples' Friendship University is founded
April 14, 1961	Moscow welcomes Yuri Gagarin, the world's first cosmonaut
1961	The Kremlin Palace of Congresses is built

Historic period or year	Event
October 1961	The 22nd Congress of the CPSU adopts the new Party Programme
October 1964	The Plenum of the CPSU Central Committee elects Leonid Brezhnev its First Secretary (General Secretary since 1966)
November 1967	The 50th anniversary of the Great October Socialist Revolution
April 1970	Centenary of the birth of Lenin
1971	The new general plan for Moscow's development is adopted
March 1971	The 24th Congress of the CPSU adopts the Peace Programme actively and consistently implemented by the Soviet Government
October 1973	The World Congress of Peace Forces meets in Moscow
February-March 1976	The 25th Congress of the CPSU takes place in Moscow. It gives concrete expression to the Party's economic policy for the next five years and over a longer period of time, and defines the new international tasks of the CPSU which arise from the Peace Programme
October 7, 1977	Special session of the USSR Supreme Soviet adopts the new Constitution of the USSR, the Fundamental Law of the developed socialist society
November 1977	The 60th anniversary of the Great October Socialist Revolution

И ДОЛГО БУДУ ТЕМ ЛЮБЕЗЕН
Я НАРОДУ,
ЧТО ЧУВСТВА ДОБРЫЕ
Я ЛИРОЙ ПРОБУЖДАЛ,
ЧТО В МОЙ ЖЕСТОКИЙ ВЕК
ВОССЛАВИЛ Я СВОБОДУ
И МИЛОСТЬ К ПАДШИМ
ПРИЗЫВАЛ.

FIRST DAY

We recommend you to begin your tour of Moscow in the morning with a visit to Red Square and the Lenin Mausoleum, and a look round the Kremlin's historic monuments and museums; and then, in the afternoon, to take a walk along Gorky Street.

The Lenin Mausoleum on Red Square is open to visitors on Tuesdays, Wednesdays, Thursdays, and Saturdays from 11:00 to 14:00 (in summer from 9:00 to 13:00), and on Sundays from 11:00 to 16:00 (in summer, from 9:00 to 14:00). Foreign tourists wishing to visit it usually assemble at the corner of the History Museum opposite the Corner Arsenal Tower of the Kremlin (facing 50th Anniversary of October Square). Militia officers let them through in a separate queue on Tuesdays, Wednesdays, Thursdays and Saturdays from 12:00 to 13:00 and on Sundays from 13:00 to 14:00. The nearest Metro stations are Ploshchad Revolutsii and Prospekt Marxa, using the exit into Gorky Street.

The Kremlin and its museums are open to visitors daily, except Thursdays, from 10:00 to 18:00. The way into the Kremlin is through the Troitsky and Borovitsky gates. The nearest Metro station is Biblioteka imeni Lenina. Entry to the Kremlin is free; tickets for the museums cost 15 kopecks each, except to the Armoury, for which they cost 30 kopecks (or 40 kopecks with a guide). We advise you to visit the Armoury with one of the excursions that can be booked through the hotel service bureau or at Intourist's Central Excursion Bureau.

Please note that it is not permitted to enter either the Lenin Mausoleum or the Kremlin carrying a briefcase, carrier bag, parcel, and so on. Any of the monuments within the Kremlin may be photographed, but not the interiors of the museums. It is customary to remove one's headgear inside the museums and, of course, to refrain from smoking.

RED SQUARE

Everyone visiting Moscow for the first time probably begins his acquaintance with the city at Red Square *(Krasnaya Ploshchad)*, which is only to be expected as Red Square is the heart of Moscow.

By the Kremlin wall in Red Square is the **Lenin Mausoleum.** Inside it, in a crystal sarcophagus, lies the body of Vladimir Ilyich Lenin, the great revolutionary and founder of the Communist Party of the Soviet Union and of the Soviet state, who died on January 21, 1924. Originally there was a wooden Mausoleum, erected in three days. In May 1924 it was rebuilt and then in 1930 it was replaced by the present granite and marble Mausoleum, designed by the architect Alexei Shchusev. A large monolith above the main portal bears the laconic inscription LENIN, incrusted in dark red porphyry.

On the days the Mausoleum is open to the public people can be seen moving slowly toward it from the Alexandrovsky Gardens. In summer or winter, rain or shine, hail or snow, there is always a queue on Red Square.

For more than fifty years now an endless stream of Muscovites, and of those who come to Moscow, including visitors from abroad, have wended their way across Red Square to the Mausoleum.

A guard of honour stands at the entrance. The changing of the guard (on the hour every hour) attracts the onlookers by its ceremonial precision.

At both sides of the Mausoleum along the side of Red Square there are marble stands, and behind them, along the Kremlin wall, stand stately spruces, motionless as sentinels.

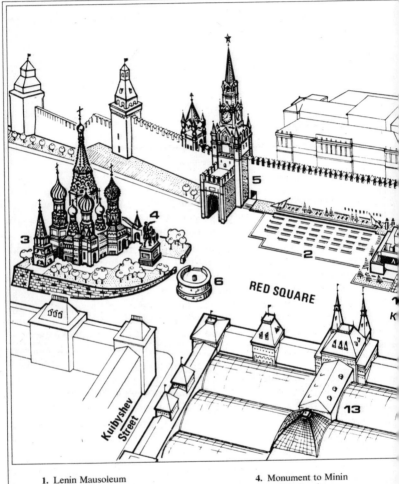

RED SQUARE

Kuibyshev Street

1. Lenin Mausoleum
2. Marble Stands
3. St. Basil's Cathedral (Cathedral of the Intercession)
4. Monument to Minin and Pozharsky
5. Spasskaya Tower
6. Lobnoye Mesto

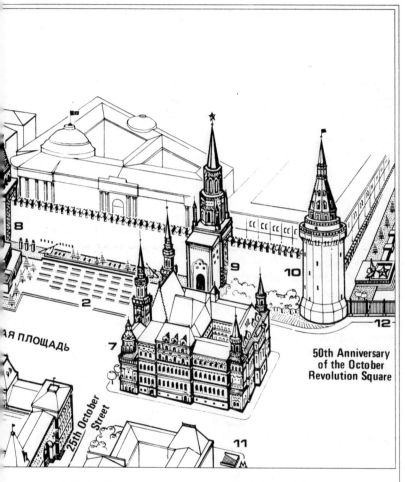

ПЛОЩАДЬ

25th October Street

**50th Anniversary
of the October
Revolution Square**

7. History Museum
8. Senate Tower
9. Nikolskaya Tower
10. Corner Arsenal Tower

11. Underpass to Prospekt Marxa
    Metro station
12. Alexandrovsky Gardens
13. State Department Store (GUM)

Many memorable events in the country's history are associated with Red Square. It is first mentioned in 15th-century chronicles. Nearly all the roads leading to Moscow from all ends of Russia converged there. It was the place to learn news, and the starting point of many riots and revolts of the working people against their oppressors.

A deep moat ran along the Kremlin wall at one time separating it from Red Square. The square itself received its present name in the 17th century from the Russian word *krasny*, meaning "fair, beautiful".

This old square has witnessed many historic events. Here ceremonies were performed, victories celebrated, funerals and national celebrations held. Here, too, the tsarist executioners beheaded the leaders of popular revolts.

In the autumn of 1917 there was fierce fighting on Red Square between the forces of the Revolution and those of reaction. Its cobblestones were stained with the blood of revolutionary workers and soldiers, and its name acquired a new and deeper meaning.

Lenin spoke on Red Square many times, passionately calling on the people to uphold the socialist revolution and the freedom and independence of the Soviet land, to defend it against intervention, to help put an end to wars between nations, and to build a new, communist society.

Lenin first spoke in Red Square on November 7, 1918, the first anniversary of the Great October Socialist Revolution, at the unveiling of a memorial plaque on the Kremlin's Senate Tower in memory of those who died fighting for the October Revolution. (In 1950, when the tower was restored, the plaque was removed and transferred to the Museum of the Revolution.)

It was here, on Red Square, during the May Day demonstration in 1919, that Lenin said: "Up to now the story of what our children would see in the future has sounded like a fairy-tale; but today, comrades, you clearly see that the edifice of socialist society, of which we have laid the foundations, is not a utopia. Our children will build this edifice with even greater zeal."

Red Square is the site of Moscow's annual demonstrations on the May Day and November 7 national holidays, when representatives of its working people march past the Mausoleum and the stands where guests from all the Union Republics and other countries are assembled, reporting their labour achievements, expressing their dedication to the cause of building communism in the USSR, and demonstrating their desire to live in peace with all the peoples on earth.

On November 7, 1941, when nazi troops were approaching Moscow, Soviet soldiers marched past the Lenin Mausoleum during the annual revolutionary parade, pledging to defend the capital to the last.

On June 24, 1945, the historic Victory Parade was held on the square in commemoration of the defeat of Hitler Germany. To the roll of drums, Soviet soldiers cast two hundred enemy standards at the foot of the Mausoleum, standards captured by Soviet troops in the field of battle.

The people have long since honoured their heroes in Red Square. On April 14, 1961 there was a special occasion when Soviet people celebrated an outstanding event, the first manned space flight in the world by the Soviet cosmonaut, Yuri Gagarin. Since then Red Square has ceremoniously welcomed his comrades, other cosmonauts, including Valentina Nikolayeva-Tereshkova, the world's first woman to enter space.

Every year in June, after their last day at secondary school, boys and girls come to Red Square and make it resound with their songs, laughter and happy voices.

After visiting the Lenin Mausoleum you can go along the Kremlin wall. By it are the common graves of the workers and soldiers who died in October 1917 fighting for Soviet power. And immediately behind the Mausoleum are the tombstones on the graves of outstanding leaders of the Communist Party and Soviet statesmen. Here, too, are buried renowned workers of the international Communist movement: Clara Zetkin, Sen Katayama, John Reed and Fritz Heckert.

Red Square, one of the most beautiful squares in the world, is 695 metres long and has an average width of up to 130 metres and an area of more than 70,000 square metres. In 1930 it was paved with stone blocks.

The architectural ensemble of Red Square developed gradually, over the centuries.

In 1555-61 **St. Basil's Cathedral** (the **Cathedral of the Intercession**), a unique creation of Russian national art, was built on the square. It was erected on the order of Ivan IV (the Terrible) to commemorate the annexation of the Kazan and Astrakhan khanates to Russia.

The names of the builders had been forgotten for over three centuries, and it was only in 1896 that some old manuscripts were discovered that mentioned the "Russian masters Posnik and Barma", by whose genius this architectural masterpiece was created.

The Cathedral of the Intercession consists of nine pillar-like chapels united by a single artistic idea, yet each quite unlike the others. In the centre the tallest central chapel rises to a height of 57 metres and is crowned by a bright hipped roof. In 1588 a small chapel was erected next to the Cathedral over the grave of a certain Vassily, a God's fool well-known in Moscow at that time. Ever since the Cathedral of the Intercession has been known as the Church of Vassily the Blessed, or St. Basil's Cathedral.

The Cathedral is built of brick in traditional Russian style; at the same time it contains many elements of old Russian wooden architecture. Inside the Cathedral some remarkable 16th century frescoes are preserved, which Soviet experts discovered during restoration work begun in 1954.

The interior of each of the chapels is as individual as its exterior. The inner gallery contains fine wall and ceiling paintings (17th century)—a wonderful pattern of flowers of unique shapes, mainly in red and turquoise. There is also a 16th-century icon *Entering Jerusalem*, one of the best examples of the Moscow school. The iconostasis with its 16th- and 17th-century painting is one of the oldest works of Russian art preserved in the Cathedral.

Restoration work is still going on in the Cathedral. Most of the old Russian paintings, long concealed under later layers of oil paint, have already been restored to their original appearance. Marvellous frescoes dating from the time of Ivan the Terrible again amaze and gladden the eye.

The beauty and splendour of the Cathedral gave rise to a popular legend. Word had it that Ivan the Terrible asked the builders whether they could build anything finer or duplicate what they had already done. When they answered that they could, he ordered them in a rage to be blinded so that there would never be anything more beautiful in the world than the Cathedral of the Intercession.

A branch of the History Museum has been opened in the Cathedral with exhibits tracing the history of this remarkable monument of Russian architecture and Ivan IV's campaign against Kazan.

The museum is open daily (except Tuesdays) from 9:30 to 17:00. Admission 20 kopecks.

Next to the Cathedral stands the **monument to Minin and Pozharsky*, the first civil monument erected in Moscow and one of the finest in Russia. It was sculptured by Ivan Martos in classical style and depicts the historic meeting of Kozma Minin, the elder of Nizhny Novgorod, and Prince Dmitry Pozharsky. Under the leadership of these two heroes of the 1612 war of liberation, the people's volunteers drove the Polish invaders out of Moscow and upheld the independence of the Russian state. No portraits made of Kozma Minin and Dmitry Pozharsky in their lifetime had been preserved, so the sculptor gave them the typical features of the finest Russian people of the time—strong-willed, courageous people with a boundless love for their country. The inscription on the pedestal reads: "To Citizen Minin and Prince Pozharsky from a grateful Russia 1818". Martos's sculpture, erected with money raised by public subscription, became a truly national monument.

Near St. Basil's Cathedral is the ****Spasskaya** (Saviour) **Tower**, the main and tallest tower of the Kremlin, which has long since become one of the symbols of Moscow. This majestic, graceful tower was built in 1491 by Russian crafts- men under the supervision of the Italian architect Pietro

Antonio Solari of Milan. It acquired its present appearance in 1624-25 when the Russian architect Bazhen Ogurtsov completed it with an octagonal multi-storey spire. In those days ceremonial processions of the clergy passed through the Spassky Gate, and tsars, emperors, and foreign ambassadors drove into the Kremlin through it. It was forbidden to ride through it on horseback or to pass through with one's head covered; even the tsars were required to remove their hats.

The first clock was presumably mounted on the Spasskaya Tower in 1491, and remained there until 1625, when it was replaced by a new one. In 1851-52 the Kremlin Chimes, ten bells cast in the 17th-18th centuries, were installed. The chime mechanism occupies three floors. The clockface is 6.12 metres in diameter and each figure is 72 centimetres high. The hour hand is 2.97 metres long, and the minute hand 3.28 metres. The clock itself weighs 25 tons.

During the storming of the Kremlin in the October battles of 1917, the clock was damaged by artillery fire. In 1918, however, it was restored on Lenin's instructions by Nikolai Berens. In 1974 the unique mechanism was completely renovated. The chimes are broadcast daily by Radio Moscow at 6:00 and midnight.

Not far from the Cathedral of the Intercession in Red Square is what is called the **Lobnoye Mesto**, or Place of Execution, a platform of white stone more than 400 years old. The tsar's edicts were proclaimed here and public executions carried out.

Behind the cathedral, just beyond Red Square, is the *Rossia Hotel, designed by Dmitry Chechulin. It contains 3,200 rooms and can accommodate some 6,000 guests. Automated artificial climate control is in operation, there is a dust-cleaner system, and various other electronic equipment has been installed to ensure that the service personnel provide maximum comfort for the guests of the capital. The hotel has several restaurants, one with a floor show every night. In addition there are some 30 bars, snack-bars and cafes on various floors. The 21-storey tower is the compositional centre of the hotel. It contains some very comfortable suites, ranging in size from one room to five. The restaurant on the top floor of this block has the best service and decor, and a marvellous view of Red Square and the Kremlin from its wide windows 80 metres up.

The building of the hotel also houses the USSR Ministry of Culture's **Concert Hall** (seating 2,600) and the **Zaryadye Cinema** (box offices and entrances on the Moskva River side).

The erection of such a big hotel close to the Kremlin gave the architects a very responsible job, for they had to blend it into the skyline of the city centre with its ensemble of precious monuments of Russian architecture, so that past and present would complement and enrich each other. They coped with the task beautifully. A number of small churches alongside the hotel were carefully preserved as rare cultural monuments during the reconstruction of this area, and fit in well against the hotel. One of them, St. Anne's, between the hotel and the river, is the same age as the Kremlin walls, having been built at the end of the 15th century during the reign of Ivan III.

But let us return to Red Square, and walk up from St. Basil's to the opposite end. We are now facing a red brick building with four pairs of dissimilar towers. This is the *His**tory Museum**, founded on the initiative of many prominent progressives of the last century. It was built in 1878-83 to the plans of Vladimir Sherwood, member of the Academy of Arts, on the site of the two-storey building in which Moscow University was founded in 1755 by Mikhail Lomonosov, the great Russian scientist. Before the Revolution the Museum was supported by private donations, and had around 300,000 exhibits. Today it is a major depository of documents and relics relating to the history of the peoples of the USSR. It contains around four million objects and there are 44,000 files in its archives. The Museum and its branches in St. Basil's and the Novodevichy Convent are visited annually by more than two million people.

The exhibits in the Museum's 48 halls introduce the visitor to the history of the peoples of the USSR from the Stone Age to the present. It houses the country's largest archaeological collection, a unique collection of coins and medals, collections of precious ornaments and household articles, old manuscripts and books, many original historical documents, and a fine collection of works of art. The exhibits include letters written on birch bark in 10th-century Novgorod; clothes worn by Tsar Ivan the Terrible; Peter the Great's sleigh; a portrait of Emelyan Pugachev, leader of 18th-century Peasants' War, painted over a portrait of Empress Catherine II; Napoleon's sabre and field kitchen captured at Vyazma by a Russian cavalry detachment in 1812; the spyglass of the great Russian general Mikhail Kutuzov; fetters, put on peoples who rebelled against the tsarist autocracy; the first issue of the revolutionary newspaper *Kolokol* (The Bell), published by Alexander Herzen and Nikolai Ogarev, which played an immense role in the history of the revolutionary movement in Russia; and the first decree of Soviet power, the Decree on Peace, written by Lenin.

The History Museum is open on Mondays, Thursdays, Saturdays, and Sundays from 10:00 to 18:00, and on Wednesdays and Fridays from 11:00 to 19:00. It is closed on Tuesdays and on the first Monday of every month. Admission 20 kopecks.

To the left of the History Museum stands the graceful three-tiered ***Nikolskaya** (St. Nicholas) **Tower** built in 1491 by Pietro Antonio Solari. It was through the Nikolsky and Spassky gates that the people's volunteers led by Minin and Pozharsky fought their way into the Kremlin in 1612 to oust the Polish invaders encamped there. And it was through the same gates that the revolutionary forces broke into the Kremlin in 1917 and crushed counter-revolutionary resistance. A memorial plaque on the History Museum commemorates this event.

The architectural originality of the Nikolskaya Tower is to be seen in its Gothic lacework decorations of the façade; its whitestone openwork elements and tall hipped roof, erected at the beginning of the 19th century, are by the architect Ruska. The roof and part of the tower were destroyed by Napoleon's retreating troops in 1812, but were restored in 1816 to plans prepared by the architect Beauvais.

The tower was badly damaged again by artillery fire during the storming of the Kremlin in 1917, and was restored on Lenin's instruction by Nikolai Morkovnikov. Its height, including the ruby-red star, is 70.4 metres.

Opposite the Kremlin, along the whole length of Red Square stretches the two-storeyed building with plateglass show windows of the **State Department Store** (GUM), the biggest in the USSR. The building, originally known as the Upper Trading Stalls, was designed by architect Alexander Pomerantsev and erected in 1895. Before the Revolution it contained around 200 small shops. In 1953 the building was completely reconstructed, with booths and counters of a total length of 2.5 kilometres. It handles some 350,000 customers every day.

In 1974 extensive restoration and maintenance work was carried out on Red Square; the Lenin Mausoleum and stands were renovated, a memorial complex was built on the grave of the fighters for the Revolution, and the stone blocks of the square were relaid. The Moscow builders were helped by workers from many parts of the country. Red and grey granite was sent from the Ukraine, grey basalt from Karelia, special clay for the bricks from the Baltic area, and limestone from the Crimea.

We leave Red Square through Istorichesky Proyezd, leading us to the underground crossing and Prospekt Marxa Metro station. On our right is the building of the ****Central Lenin Museum,** which houses unique materials and documents on the life of the great leader of the proletariat.

Behind the museum is the Ploshchad Revolutsii Metro station.

But let us turn left to the grilles of the gates of the ****Alexandrovsky Gardens.** Inside the gates, by the Kremlin wall, is the ****Tomb of the Unknown Soldier**, before which burns an eternal flame. On its granite plinth are the following words: "Thy name is unknown, thy feat immortal." The remains of the Unknown Soldier were brought here from the forty-first kilometre along Leningrad Highway where, in the grim days of November 1941, the front line passed and where the Soviet soldiers and Moscow volunteers detachments halted the enemy. The monument was unveiled on May 8, 1967 by the General Secretary of the Central Committee of the Communist Party, Leonid Brezhnev.

It is symbolic that the flame of glory that burns here was brought from the sacred Field of Mars in Leningrad, where the heroes of the Great October Socialist Revolution are buried.

Along the alley in front of the Tomb of the Unknown Soldier stand blocks of red porphyry with earth from the Hero Cities of Leningrad,

Odessa, Sevastopol, Volgograd, Kiev, Minsk, Novorossiisk, Kerch, Tula, and the Brest Fortress.

The Soviet people achieved victory in the Second World War at a vast price. Soviet troops fought for victory for 1,418 days. Twenty million people lost their lives. They fell in battle or died in death camps and in the flames of towns and villages burnt by fascist punitive expeditions. Seven hundred thousand Muscovites fought at the front during the war. Many Moscow families lost a loved, a father, brother, sister, or son. Every year on May 9, Victory Day, the whole country honours its dead with a minute of silence, and flowers are laid on the soldiers' graves and memorials. This tradition is also observed by young married couples who come to the Tomb of the Unknown Soldier on their wedding day to express their gratitude to those who died to defend their lives, their freedom, and their happiness.

Now let us walk along the Kremlin wall deeper into the Alexandrovsky Gardens. They were laid out in 1820-21; it is interesting to note that the Neglinnaya River flows under them in a pipe. The gardens are a favourite spot with Muscovites and guests to the capital.

Lev Tolstoy, the great novelist, was extremely fond of the Kremlin from his childhood and used to enjoy walking in the Alexandrovsky Gardens. In a school essay he once wrote: "What a magnificent sight the Kremlin is! The dawn of Russia's liberation arose over these walls."

If you come to Moscow in summer, we advise you, too, to take a stroll along its shady alleys or by its large flowerbeds, which have magnificent displays from early spring to late autumn.

Opposite the **Middle Arsenal** (Srednyaya Arsenalnaya) **Tower** and its grotto—a memorial to the 1812 Patriotic War—beside the central alley, stands a granite obelisk, on which, on Lenin's instructions, are inscribed the names of great revolutionaries and thinkers: Karl Marx, Frederick Engels, Karl Liebknecht, Ferdinand Lassalle, August Bebel, Tommaso Campanella, Jan Meslier, Gerrard Winstanely, Thomas More, Henry Claude Saint-Simon, Charles Fourier, Jean Jaurès, Pierre Joseph Proudhon, Mikhail Bakunin, Nikolai Chernyshevsky, Pyotr Lavrov, Nikolai Mikhailovsky, and Georgi Plekhanov. This, the first monument of revolutionary Russia, was unveiled in 1918.

The central alley of the Alexandrovsky Gardens leads to Troitsky Bridge, embellished, like the Kremlin walls, with V-shaped merlons and loopholes. This bridge joins the Troitskaya and Kutafya towers, through which one may enter the Kremlin.

THE KREMLIN

What is the best way to look round the Kremlin? You can, if you wish, walk right along its crenellated walls, which run around the Kremlin for 2,235 metres. Or you can begin by looking at it from Maurice Thorez Embankment, or Moskvoretsky or Bolshoi Kamenny bridges, from which you get a good view of the cathedrals, the Grand Kremlin Palace, and the Kremlin walls and towers. Alternatively, you may view it first from Red Square or from 50th Anniversary of the October Revolution Square (formerly Manège Square), the National or Rossia hotels. In fact, it is worth viewing the Kremlin from all of these vantage points so as to see its various perspectives. But nothing, of course, can equal a walk inside the Kremlin itself.

> After visiting Moscow, Emile Verhaeren, the eminent Belgian poet, said: "The whole city looks like a huge open-air museum to me; and the most perfect, the most unique, and the most attractive sight is the Kremlin.
>
> "Walled in by vast embattlements, the Kremlin, where hundreds of cupolas protrude, looking just like the necks and beaks of golden birds straining towards the light, remains in my mind's eye the most beautiful fairyland scene I have ever seen."

This outstanding monument of Russian history and culture stands majestically on a steep elevation overlooking the Moskva River, and covers an area of 28 hectares.

We recommend you to begin your sightseeing tour of the Kremlin by entering through the Troitskaya Tower, which is not far from Biblioteka imeni Lenina and Kalininskaya Metro stations.

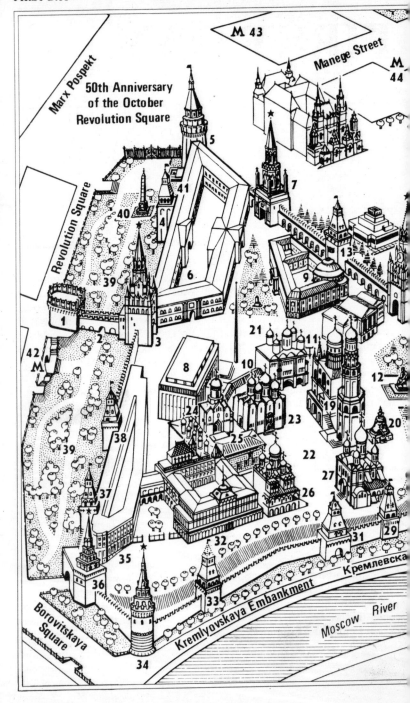

Marx Pospekt

50th Anniversary
of the October
Revolution Square

M 43

Manege Street

M 44

Revolution Square

5

41

40

4

39

6

7

13

9

1

2

3

21

42
M

8

10

11

12

24

19

38

23

39

25

20

37

22

27

26

32

35

31

29

36

33

34

Borovitskaya
Square

Kremlyovskaya Embankment

Кремлевска

Moscow River

1. Kutafya Tower (entry to the Kremlin)
2. Troitsky Bridge
3. Troitskaya Tower
4. Middle Arsenal Tower
5. Corner Arsenal Tower
6. Arsenal
7. Nikolskaya Tower
8. Kremlin Palace of Congresses
9. Building of the former Senate
10. Patriarch's Palace and Church of the Twelve Apostles. Museum of 17th-century life and applied art
11. Tsar-Cannon
12. Statue of Lenin
13. Senate Tower
14. Spasskaya Tower
15. Tsar's Tower
16. Konstantino-Yeleninskaya Tower
17. Nabatnaya Tower
18. Moskvoretskaya (Beklemishevskaya) Tower
19. Ivan the Great Bell Tower and Belfry
20. Tsar-Bell
21. Ivan Square
22. Cathedral Square
23. Cathedral of the Assumption
24. Church of the Deposition of the Robe
25. Palace of Facets
26. Cathedral of the Annunciation
27. Archangel Cathedral
28. Peter's Tower
29. 1st Nameless Tower
30. 2nd Nameless Tower
31. Tainitskaya Tower
32. Grand Kremlin Palace
33. Annunciation Tower
34. Vodovzvodnaya Tower
35. Armoury
36. Borovitskaya Tower (entrance to the Kremlin)
37. Armoury Tower
38. Commandant's Tower
39. Alexandrovsky Gardens
40. Obelisk to the great revolutionaries and thinkers
41. Tomb of the Unknown Soldier
42. Biblioteka imeni Lenina Metro station. Arbatskaya & Kalininskaya Metro stations
43. Prospekt Marksa Metro station
44. Sverdlov Square & Revolution Square Metro stations

Near the tall Troitskaya Tower, built of red brick with white-stone loopholes, is a monumental structure of concrete and glass the upper floors of which rise above the Kremlin walls. This is the Palace of Congresses, the most modern building in the Kremlin.

The first structure we pass through is the *Kutafya Tower built in the early 16th century as the bridgehead watchtower. Then it was surrounded by a moat and approached by drawbridges. From this tower runs a stone bridge with crenellated parapets, under which the Neglinnaya River used to flow.

The *Troitskaya (Trinity) Tower was erected in 1495. It is six storeys high and has a deep, two-storey basement, where ammunition used to be stored for the Kremlin's defence. It is the tallest of the Kremlin towers, and is 80 metres high to the top of its star. Tsars and military commanders returning victorious from campaigns used to ride into the Kremlin either through the Troitsky Gate or through the Spassky Gate. It was also through the Troitsky Gate that Napoleon's troops entered, and later fled from the Kremlin.

In March 1918 Lenin, as head of the first Soviet Government, entered the Kremlin through the Troitsky Gate.

Vladimir Bonch-Bruyevich, who was then office manager of the Council of People's Commissars, described the event as follows:

"It was a sunny spring day when at twelve o'clock, we drew up to the Troitsky Gate leading to the Kremlin. The sentries, of course, stopped us. We showed our passes. The commander of the guard on duty that day came up in full military dress, and asked:

"'Who goes there?'

"'The Chairman of the Council of People's Commissars, Vladimir Ilyich Lenin,' I replied. The officer took two steps back and stood to attention, looking at Lenin. The latter smiled, raised his hand to his round, astrakhan hat, and saluted.

"We drove smoothly through the old gate."

Bonch-Bruyevich recalled that Lenin, while looking round the Kremlin, was interested whether they had managed to preserve the objects of value in the Armoury, the palaces, particularly in the Palace of Facets, and the famous Patriarch's Vestry and Library with its priceless books and manuscripts.

The Kremlin is the oldest historical and architectural centre of Moscow. The old chronicles record that in the year 1147 Prince Yuri Dolgoruky of Suzdal met Prince Svyatoslav of Chernigov-Seversky on Borovitsky Hill (now called Kremlin Hill). This is the first written mention of Moscow. Recent excavations in the Kremlin, however, which discovered remnants of old structures, lead us to believe that its area was inhabited as early as the 11th century, that is, well before the generally accepted date of the city's foundation.

In 1156 Prince Yuri Dolgoruky ordered a wooden fort to be built on Borovitsky Hill, which later became the residence of the Apanage Prince of Moscow. That was when the building of the Kremlin began.

This fortress was razed to the ground in 1238 during the Tatar invasion; but Moscow continued to live and grow. In 1326-39 walls of oak were erected around the Kremlin. Two cathedrals built of stone, the Archangel Cathedral and the Cathedral of the Assumption—the forerunners of the present cathedrals—rose among the wooden structures. The Kremlin became the residence of the Grand Princes and Metropolitans of Moscow. The oak walls were replaced by white-stone ones and towers in 1367-68 and Moscow began to be called a white-stone town. In 1382 the Tatar Khan Tokhtamysh and his hordes broke into the Kremlin through undefended gates, demolished the fortress, pillaged the churches, burnt the houses inside it, and killed around half the population. Moscow had to start building all over again.

In 1485-95, during the reign of Ivan III, the walls of white stone, which had survived many fires and sieges over a hundred years or so, were replaced by new brick walls and towers, and these, restored many times, are those still standing. At the same time the area of the Kremlin was extended to its present size. Skilled craftsmen were brought from all the corners of Russia, from Pskov and Vladimir, from Novgorod and Tver, to replace the old cathedrals, built over a century earlier, with new ones. By the order of Ivan III the famous Italian architects Aristotile Fioravante, Pietro Antonio Solari, Marco Ruffo, and Alevisio Novi were invited to work in Moscow. The results of the joint work of Russian craftsmen and these fine architects were wonderful structures that amaze everyone who sees them.

The consolidation of the Russian state in the 17th century was accompanied by a flourishing of national art and architecture.

In 1712 the capital was moved from Moscow to St. Petersburg. The Kremlin became the temporary residence of the tsar's court. Russian emperors and empresses came here to be crowned, to pay their respects to their ancestors and pray at the shrines of the Kremlin. The life of the Kremlin seemed to quieten but a new misfortune awaited it. In 1737 a great fire destroyed all the wooden structures still standing within it. Building began once more.

The Kremlin also suffered greatly in the Patriotic War of 1812. In September of that year Napoleon's armies marched into Moscow, which had been abandoned by its inhabitants and the Russian army. For a month and four days French troops were quartered in the Kremlin. When forced to retreat from Moscow they tried, on Napoleon's orders, to blow up the Kremlin; but thanks to the courage of the Cossacks and the townsfolk who had remained behind in the city, they failed to achieve their criminal design. At the risk of their lives the people extinguished many of the burning fuses; but still some of the powder trains worked and caused considerable damage. Three towers and the belfry of the Ivan the Great Bell Tower were destroyed, and the Nikolskaya Tower and other structures severely damaged. After the war, however, everything was restored.

In the 19th century the Kremlin was enriched by new structures, the Grand Palace and the new building of the Armoury.

In the 20th century a new era in the history of the Moscow Kremlin began. In March 1918 the Soviet Government moved to Moscow from Petrograd and the Kremlin became its permanent seat, and Moscow, the capital of the first socialist state in the world.

Here, in 1918, Lenin signed a decree on the protection of works of art and historic monuments. "The beautiful must be preserved, and taken as a model and used as a starting point, even though it is 'old'," he wrote. In keeping with this decree, all the monuments of the past, cultural and artistic, including the Kremlin, were placed under state protection, and restoration work began in the Kremlin.

In 1937 glowing ruby-red stars, designed by Academician Fyodor Fyodorovsky, were mounted on the five tallest towers. From below they do not seem large, but in fact the span of the smallest of them, on the Vodovzvodnaya Tower, is nearly three metres, and it weighs a ton. The largest stars are on the Nikolskaya and Spasskaya towers with a span of 3.75 metres and weigh one and a half tons.

Restoration work was resumed in 1945, right after the Second World War. Dilapidated sections of the walls and towers were replaced. The tops of the towers were retiled and covered with sheet copper, and the walls given a damp-proof coating to protect them against the weather. By 1955 all the cathedrals and the Palace of Facets had been fully repaired, the old stone pavement of Cathedral Square restored, and the dome of the Ivan the Great Bell Tower regilded. Restoration work is still going on in the Kremlin today. In 1974 the towers overlooking Red Square were restored and their stars renewed, and in 1975 it was the turn of the Kutafya, Troitskaya and Corner Arsenal towers.

Now let us continue our excursion. Inside the walls, to the right of the Troitskaya Tower is the **Palace of Congresses.** This monumental building was erected on the site of several service buildings of no historic value. The builders realised how difficult it would be to organically inscribe a modern structure in an ensemble of magnificent architectural monuments of different epochs.

They succeeded in doing so, however. In 1961 a building in Urals marble, glass, and aluminium, with expressive, yet austere lines, was erected to the designs of a team of Soviet architects and engineers headed by Mikhail Posokhin. Its white marble pylons and glass panels give it a light, festive, and majestic appearance.

Although extremely complex as regards architecture and construction, the Palace was built in a very short time, just over a year. The government esteemed the builders' work highly and many of them were awarded orders and medals. A group of designers and builders were given the country's highest award, the Lenin Prize, awarded annually on Lenin's birthday for the best works in literature, art, science, and engineering.

A feature of the Palace of Congresses is that it is sunk 15 metres into the ground. It contains 800 rooms and halls. Its five storeys are connected by wide staircases and 14 escalators. The walls and columns are faced with marble and tufas from Georgia, Armenia, Siberia, and the Urals.

The huge, but simple, handsome auditorium seats 6,000. The white aluminium strips on the ceiling are arranged in the shape of the rows of seats.

Above the auditorium there is a buffet and banquet hall for 2,500 people. The hall is, as it were, suspended on steel springs, which improves its sound insulation. There is a wonderful view of Moscow and the Kremlin's old churches from its huge glass windows.

Party and trade union congresses, international conferences and festivals, and public meetings are held here. The auditorium is also used for concerts, and for ballets and operas staged by the Bolshoi Theatre.

In the spring of 1976 the 25th Congress of the Soviet Communist Party took place in the Kremlin Palace of Congresses. It was attended by 103 delegations of communist, workers', national-democratic and socialist parties from 96 countries.

The 25th Congress specified the fundamental lines of the Party's economic policy under developed socialism for the next five years and over a longer period and defined the new international tasks of the CPSU, which arise from the Peace Programme adopted at the 24th Congress.

At its first Plenum after the 25th Congress the Central Committee of the CPSU again elected Leonid Brezhnev as its General Secretary. In 1977 he was elected Chairman of the Presidium of the USSR Supreme Soviet.

After looking at the Palace of Congresses from the outside, we suggest that you see its interior, too, which you can do in the evening by attending a show or concert there. Tickets should be booked in advance through the service bureau in your hotel.

Now let us continue our tour of the sights of the Kremlin.

Along the wall, to the left of the Troitskaya Tower as you come in, stretches a two-storey building, once the *Arsenal. This building, ornamented with a carved white frieze, is over 30 metres high. The few, widely spaced, deep-set pairs of windows accentuate the thickness of the walls. The Arsenal is a splendid example of early 18th-century architecture. Work on it began in 1702 on the orders of Peter the Great, and was completed in 1736. It is believed to be mainly the work of the architects Christopher Konrad and Dmitry Ivanov.

Along the front of the Arsenal are 875 guns, trophies captured from Napoleon's army in 1812.

On both sides of the entrance there are two memorial plaques; one commemorates the revolutionary soldiers of the Kremlin Arsenal who were brutally shot on October 28, 1917 by cadets; the other bears the names of the 92 officers and men of the Kremlin garrison who died defending Moscow against nazi air raids during the Second World War.

Beyond the small garden opposite the Arsenal stands a three-storey building with a high socle and a magnificent white cornice, the windows of which on the first and second floors are divided by pilasters. This building, formerly the *Senate, was erected in 1776-88 to the designs of the architect Matvei Kazakov in the Russian classical style. On the wall of the building is a memorial plaque bearing Lenin's portrait in bas-relief and the inscription: "V. I. Lenin lived and worked in this building from March 1918 to May 1923."

It was from here that Lenin directed the defence of the Soviet state in the grim years of the Civil War and foreign intervention, and guided the country's political and economic activities during the period of economic dislocation and famine.

Lenin's study and flat were on the second floor of the building. Everything in it is kept exactly as it was in Lenin's time. The furnishings are very modest. In the room in which Lenin lived there is a small desk with a simple desk-set. It was here that Lenin, already gravely ill, wrote his last five works: *Pages from a Diary, On Co-operation, Our Revolution, How We Should Reorganise the Workers' and Peasants' Inspection,* and *Better Fewer, But Better,* which were his political testament to the Communist Party and the Soviet people.

In the study Lenin received delegates from distant villages, workers' delegations, and guests from abroad. There, too, he signed many decrees.

A special door leads from the office to a hall where the Council of People's Commissars used to meet. The armchair used by Lenin stands here, preserved as a sacred relic. The conference hall and all the rooms occupied by the Council of People's Commissars in Lenin's lifetime are now a museum.

Opposite the former Senate, to the right of the Palace of Congresses is the small five-domed **Church of the Twelve Apostles** and the **Patriarch's Palace** built in 1635-56 by the Russian architects Antip Konstantinov and David Okhlebinin.

Many structures in the Patriarch's Palace have preserved their original appearance to our day. Much restoration work has been carried out here in recent years, and the Patriarch's Palace and the Church of the Twelve Apostles now house a **Museum of 17th-Century Life and Applied Art**, with over 700 exhibits of unique copper, tin, and silver articles, fabrics, and jewellery. There is also an interesting display of rare manuscripts and printed books, among them a collection of moral tales entitled *Spiritual Medicine* illustrated with 335 magnificent miniatures drawn in pen and water colours. Also on exhibit is an ABC written in 1693. Two of the halls represent the interior of a 17th-century house; each exhibit in them can be justly considered a work of art. There is also a display of Russian embroidery and gold brocade.

The main hall of the Patriarch's Palace, the Krestovaya Chamber, with a stone vault unsupported by pillars, is of impressive dimensions (its area is 280 square metres). It was built in 1653-56. The stove for preparing chrism, with its silver cauldrons and carved ornamental canopy, has been carefully preserved. In the Church of the Twelve Apostles there is a desplay case with some interesting exhibits, one a coffer for large wine bottles made in the shape of an evangelistary, on which the central figure of the image is not Christ but Bacchus. The coffer contains 28 compartments for wine bottles, and others for tobacco and pipes. Next to it is a limewood wine ladle that can hold 100 litres. These objects belonged to the Highest and Most Jolly and Drunken Council, a society founded by Peter the Great in 1691, to poke fun at the everyday rites, rituals and customs of the past, and mainly at the religious prejudices that were holding up the carrying through of progressive reforms.

From the Church of the Twelve Apostles let us go across to the *Tsar-Cannon, a remarkable example of 16th-century military engineering and foundry work. Its 890 mm calibre makes it the largest gun in the world. It was cast in bronze by Andrei Chokhov in 1586, and is some 5.34 metres long and weighs 40 tons. The gun was never fired. Experts believe it was made for stone case-shot; the iron cannon balls beside it are purely decorative, and they were cast in the 19th century.

From here at the Tsar-Cannon there is a fine view of the southeastern part of the Kremlin and the Tainitsky (Secret) Gardens (in the triangle between the eastern and southern walls), where New Year winter fairs are held for Moscow's children. An excellent view of the gardens is obtained from Kremlin Hill, which can be visited after seeing the Tsar-Cannon.

On Kremlin Hill, the highest point in the Kremlin, stands a *statue of Lenin.

Its site was not chosen by chance, for here Lenin twice worked side by side with the Kremlin military trainees during two voluntary working Saturdays (subbotniks)–in December 1919 and May 1920. Here too, with a delegation of English workers, he watched the trainees, future Red Army commanders, drilling.

The sculptors, Vladimir Pinchuk and Sergei Speransky, depicted Lenin in a moment of repose. He seems just to have torn himself away from work and sat down on the edge of a bench to rest and breathe the fresh air of the Gardens. The monument was unveiled on November 2, 1967, on the eve of the 50th anniversary of the Great October Socialist Revolution. At the ceremony, Leonid Brezhnev said: "To those who could not understand the tremendous creative power of our revolution, Lenin seemed 'the dreamer in the Kremlin'... Yes, Lenin dreamed. Like no one else he saw the future and never lost his unwavering conviction in the victory of socialism and the triumph of communist ideals. His dreams were the dreams of a great realist, the dreams of an ardent revolutionary who saw what was hidden by time. He dreamed of a free and happy life for the people, of the flourishing of science and culture, and of new victories of the international revolutionary movement. And Lenin dedicated all his strength and all his life so that these dreams could become reality."

To the left of the statue, in the middle of an alley, stands the Cosmos Oak, planted on April 14, 1961 by Yuri Gagarin.

From this side of the gardens there is a good view of the **Spasskaya** (Saviour) **Tower.**

Just to the right of the Spasskaya Tower is the **Tsar's Tower,** a small structure with a hipped roof, built in 1680. The white-stone adornments, a gilt weather vane, and rounded pinnacles at the corners make it look like something out of a Russian fairy tale. In the old days there was a wooden tower in its place from which, legend has it, Ivan the Terrible watched executions on Red Square, hence its name, the Tsar's Tower.

Further to the right is the **Moskvoretskaya** (or **Beklemishevskaya) Tower,** a tall round structure 46.2 metres high, built in 1487 by the Italian architect Marco Ruffo. This tower took the first onslaught of Tatar hordes advancing on the Kremlin. In the 17th century it was topped with a four-storey superstructure that softened its grim appearance and gave it elegance and stateliness.

From Kremlin Hill one also has a good view of the Rossia Hotel and the 173-metre-high apartment house on Kotelnicheskaya Embankment.

The part of the Kremlin wall extending along the Moskva River embankment is also clearly visible from here. The walls are 5 to 17 metres high and 3.5 to 6.5 metres thick and are surmounted with 1,045 V-shaped merlons. When the Kremlin was besieged by enemy troops, its defenders would block the openings in the merlons with wooden shields and fire at the enemy through narrow loopholes that have been preserved to this day. In the old days the walls had a protective wooden roof that sheltered the defenders in bad weather. The roof burnt down in the 18th century and was never replaced.

In the centre of the Kremlin rises one of the most remarkable structures of 16th-century Russian architecture—the *Ivan the Great Bell Tower**, a three-tier pillar consisting of elongated, octagonal sections, one on top of the other, each progressively smaller in diameter than the one below. The bells (21 in all) hanging in the arched bays of each section are splendid examples of Russian foundry work, all being richly ornamented and each one bearing an inscription giving its history (the date when it was cast, its weight, and the name of the founder).

The white tower has a gilt dome with an inscription below it in old Slavonic noting that it was built in 1600 during the reign of Boris Godunov.

Work on the campanile, however, actually began a century earlier. The new church was built on the site of an old one by the architect Bon Fryazin in 1508. Then in 1532-43 a belfry was added by the architect Petroch the Younger, in the central embrasure of which hangs the Uspensky (Assumption) Bell weighing some 70 tons. During the reign of Boris Godunov the Ivan the Great Bell Tower was completed and crowned with a gilt dome. The gilding was renewed during restoration work in 1955. The campanile is 81 metres high, and for many years it was the tallest structure in Moscow. In days of yore it served as a church, a belfry, and the main watch-tower of the Kremlin, providing a good view of the city and the surrounding area for up to 30 kilometres around.

When retreating from Moscow in 1812, Napoleon's troops tried to blow the Bell Tower up, but only succeeded in destroying the belfry and an extension on the northern side. These were later restored by the architect Domenico Gilardi.

Many pillar-like churches were built in old Russia on the model of this tower, which were meant to symbolise the might of the centralised Russian state.

On a stone pedestal at the foot of the Bell Tower stands the *Tsar-Bell—the largest bell in the world, which weighs 200 tons and is 6.14 metres high and 6.6 metres in diameter. Next to it is a fragment weighing 11.5 tons, that split off during a fire in 1737. The Tsar-Bell is a unique example of Russian foundry work. The surface of the bell has fine relief-work depicting Russian tsars, and it also bears five icons, and two inscriptions. It was cast in 1733-35 by Ivan Matorin and his son Mikhail, and lay in its casting pit for over a hundred years. It was raised in 1836 under the supervision of Auguste Montferrand and placed where it now stands.

The square between the Tsar-Bell and the Spasskaya Tower used to be called **Ivan Square**, and here were located the judicial and government offices. On this square culprits were mercilessly flogged with rods and officials loudly proclaimed the tsar's decrees.

The Ivan the Great Bell Tower unites all the Kremlin cathedrals into a majestic architectural ensemble, which faces **Cathedral Square**, the oldest square in Moscow. It was built in the early 14th century and has ever since been the main square of the Kremlin. There the ceremonial processions were held when the tsars were invested and emperors crowned, and foreign ambassadors received.

On the northern side of Cathedral Square stands the five-domed **Cathedral of the Assumption** (*Uspensky Sobor*), the main church of the Kremlin, built in 1475-79 by Russian craftsmen under the supervision of Aristotile Fioravante, a native of Bologna invited to work in Moscow by the Grand Prince Ivan III. Fioravante carefully studied the finest examples of Russian church architecture, visiting Vladimir, Pskov, and Novgorod, and modelled his Cathedral of the Assumption on that in Vladimir, which explains why motifs of Vladimir-Suzdal architecture were used so extensively in it.

The walls are of white stone, but the vaults and drums beneath the domes are of brick. The painted portals are framed with decorative white stone. The architectural proportions of the cathedral are perfect—38 metres high, 24 metres wide, and 35.5 metres long. The interior is a spacious, lofty, bright hall with vaults supported by round pillars. The interior decoration is majestic and solemn. The walls were first painted by Russian artists in 1514. The frescoes and temperas are of exceptional artistic and historical value. Most of them are the work of 14th-17th-century Russian artists. They include the 12th-century icon of St. George, an outstanding example of old Russian painting, and the 14th-century icon of the Trinity. The icon *Our Lady of Vladimir*, an example of 11th-12th-century Byzantine painting, was the oldest work in the Cathedral; it is now on display in the Tretyakov Gallery. The old murals of the Cathedral of the Assumption were several times covered by oil painting. In 1949-50 Soviet restorers discovered and reinforced the painted layer of the original murals. The restoration work still continues.

The Cathedral contains many fine examples of early Russian applied art. Among them is the southern door covered with copper sheets on which there are twenty Biblical scenes, and Slavonic inscriptions, in gold on black lacquer. Near this entrance stands the throne of Ivan the Terrible, the first Russian tsar, a unique monument to the craftsmanship of Russian wood carvers. It dates from 1551. A shrine of bronze openwork contains the remains of Patriarch Hermogen, tortured to death by the Polish invaders in 1612, and later canonised. The shrine was cast in 1624 by Dmitry Sverchkov.

Daylight penetrates the Cathedral through narrow windows arranged in two tiers. Twelve chandeliers (17th and 19th century), eleven of gilt bronze and the central one of silver and bronze, provide an additional illumination.

The Cathedral of the Assumption was the main temple of old Russia. It was the place where tsars were invested and emperors crowned. In it, too, important state decrees were proclaimed and solemn ceremonies held. It was the burial place of Moscow metropolitans and patriarchs.

To the left of the Cathedral of the Assumption is the small, single-domed **Church of the Deposition of the Robe**, whose proportions lend it an exceptionally graceful appearance. Built by craftsmen from Pskov in 1484-85, it was the private chapel of the patriarchs but became the court chapel in 1653. The iconostasis, painted by a group of artists under the supervision of Nazari Istomin (1627), is of great artistic value.

In the heart of the courtyard by the Church of the Deposition of the Robe is the Tsarina's Golden Palace (the reception hall of the 16th-century tsarinas) and the chapels of the Terem Palace. The latter chapels were joined under one roof in 1681 and crowned with eleven gilt cupolas.

Another fine example of Russian architecture, the *Palace of Facets (Granovitaya Palata)*, overlooks Cathedral Square facing the Ivan the Great Bell Tower. The Palace of Facets is one of the oldest civil edifices in Moscow. It was built in 1487-91 by Russian craftsmen working under Marco Ruffo and Pietro Antonio Solari. As its name implies, its façade is finished in faceted white stone.

The interior consists of a spacious hall with vaults supported by a central pillar. The hall is 9 metres high and has an area of 495 square metres. In the second half of the 16th century its walls and vaults had beautiful frescoes on ecclesiastical and biblical themes. In 1668 the gifted Russian artist Simon Ushakov repainted the frescoes. These remarkable frescoes were last restored in 1949.

In the 15th and 16th centuries foreign ambassadors were received in the Palace. It was there, too, that Ivan the Terrible celebrated the conquest of Kazan in 1552 and Peter the Great marked Russia's victory over the Swedes at Poltava in 1709. Today important sessions and conferences, government receptions and other ceremonial meetings are held in it.

On the same side of Cathedral Square, but closer to the river, stands another remarkable 15th-century edifice, the **Cathedral of the Annunciation** *(Blagoveshchensky Sobor)* with nine gilt domes. It was built in 1484-89 by craftsmen from Pskov. After a fire in 1547 it was restored during the reign of Ivan the Terrible. In 1572 a porch was added (on the southeastern side), known as the Groznensky (Ivan the Terrible's) Porch. The tsar must have climbed the steps of this porch many times, for the Cathedral was the private chapel of the Russian princes and tsars, which is why its architecture and interior are more intimate than those of the Cathedral of the Assumption.

The frescoes of the Cathedral of the Annunciation are magnificent. First executed in 1508, they were redone many times over the centuries and covered with oil painting. For a long time it was thought that the old frescoes had been irretrievably lost, but in 1947-61 Soviet restorers brought them to life. The Cathedral's frescoes mainly depict themes from the Apocalypse.

The iconostasis, which was taken over from the **Church of the Annunciation** that once stood on the same site, is of exceptional artistic and historical value. Its icons were painted in 1405 by Theophanes the Greek, Andrei Rublev and Prokhor of Gorodets. Their icons are evidence of the magnificent craftsmanship of the 14th- and 15th-century Russian school.

On the pilasters of the cloisters of the Groznensky Porch are the portraits of Moscow princes, and philosophers and poets of ancient Greece and Rome, including Aristotle, Plato, Homer, and Virgil.

Another Kremlin church, the **Archangel Cathedral**, faces the Cathedral of the Annunciation. Five cupolas crown this well-proportioned white edifice. This Cathedral combines the early Russian architectural style with that of the Italian Renaissance. Outwardly it is reminiscent of a Venetian palazzo. It was built in 1505-08 under the direction of the Italian architect Alevisio Novi. The walls were painted with frescoes shortly afterwards, but in 1652 the frescoes were removed together with the plaster. The present murals, painted by Russian masters, in 1652-66, depict various aspects of Russian life at the time, vividly portraying the struggle of the Russian people for national independence. The battle scenes are painted with great skill. The stylised portraits of the Russian princes are of special interest. The murals were restored in 1953-55.

A gilt iconostasis, 13 metres high, separates the central part of the Cathedral from the altar. It contains wonderful 15th-17th-century icons by Russian masters. The icon of Archangel Michael, attributed to Andrei Rublev (15th century), is of outstanding beauty and perfection.

The Archangel Cathedral was the burial place of the Moscow princes and tsars. In it are 45 tombs with white tombstones bearing inscriptions in old Slavonic; they record, in particular, that Ivan the Terrible and his sons are buried in the Cathedral. The carved gilt-white stone canopy over the tomb of Ivan the Terrible's son Dmitry is an interesting example of early 17th-century decorative art. The oldest tomb is that of Prince Ivan Kalita, who died in 1340.

During architectural and archaeological work in the Cathedral in 1962-65, several of the tombs were opened up by permission of a special commission. From the remains of the skeleton and skull, the well-known Soviet anthropologist and sculptor Mikhail Gerasimov was able to make the first documentary portrait of Ivan the Terrible.

After seeing Cathedral Square, we leave it with the Cathedral of the Annunciation on our right. Immediately behind it stretches the *Grand Kremlin Palace (1838-49; architect Konstantin Thon), 125 metres long. The palace seems to have three storeys, for three rows of windows in fact decorate the façade; but it is actually only two-storey. The arched windows on the ground floor are separated by narrow piers. The two rows of windows on the first floor are divided by pilasters and decorated with white-stone surrounds as was customary in old Russia. The higher, central part of the building is crowned by a gilt balustrade.

The Grand Kremlin Palace was erected on the site of the Grand Prince of Moscow's old palace, the halls of which were incorporated into the huge rectangle of the new palace, which was built as the Moscow residence of the imperial family.

There are several vast halls in the Palace, but the Georgievsky (St. George) Hall deserves special mention. It is 61 metres long, 20.5 metres wide, and 17.5 metres high, and is richly ornamented with stucco mouldings and 18 convoluted zinc columns, each supporting a statue of Victory crowned with a laurel wreath, sculpted by Giovanni Vitali. In the tall niches along the walls are marble slabs engraved in gold with the names of units that distinguished themselves in battle, and of officers and men awarded the Order of St. George. The hall is illuminated by six bronze gilt chandeliers in which burn 3,000 electric bulbs. The parquet is made of different coloured woods of 20 valuable varieties.

The Georgievsky Hall is used for state receptions and official ceremonies. The reception to mark victory over nazi Germany was held here in 1945. It was also here that Yuri Gagarin received his Gold Star of Hero of the Soviet Union in 1961. For years it was a tradition to hold in this hall New Year parties for Moscow schoolchildren during their winter school holidays (today these parties are held in the Palace of Congresses).

Next to the Georgievsky Hall is the octagonal **Vladimirsky** (St. Vladimir) **Hall**, which is connected with the Terem Palace, the Tsarina's Golden Palace, and the Palace of Facets. The Terem Palace was built in 1635-36 by Bazhen Ogurtsov, Antip Konstantinov, Trefil Sharutin, and Larion Ushakov, and is a rare example of 17th-century Russian architecture. Walls and ceilings are covered with colourful painting dating from 1831. The windows are glazed with stained glass. There are tiled stoves in the corners. These royal chambers evoke pictures of a dim and distant past. The Throne Room, which was the tsar's study in the 17th century, is interesting. Its middle window was called the Petition Window. From it a box used to be lowered into which anyone could put a written petition to the tsar. Among the common people, it was known as the Long Box, since petitions would lie in it for a long time, unread by anyone (which gave rise to a saying, "Never trust your business to the long box").

The largest hall in the Grand Palace has a seating capacity of 3,000 and is used for the sessions of the USSR Supreme Soviet. Its two tiers of windows overlook the Moskva River. A statue of Lenin by Sergey Merkurov stands in a niche on the platform behind the seats of the presidium.

On the ground floor of the palace, to the left of the main entrance, are suites of rooms, the Private Chambers, that used to be the imperial family's private apartments. All the rooms—the dining-room, drawing-room, empress's and emperor's studies, bedroom, and reception room—are sumptuously decorated with marble, stucco moulding and murals, and furnished with statues, porcelain and finely incrusted gilt furniture. The furnishings of these rooms have been preserved as specimens of the art of 19th-century Russian craftsmen.

Next to the Grand Palace is the **Armoury** *(Oruzheinaya Palata)*, which was built in 1851 by Konstantin Thon. The Armoury itself, however, was founded in the 16th century. It then consisted of workshops where armour and weapons were made and stored. Later, military trophies and royal regalia were preserved there. In the 17th century, on the instructions of Peter I all the historic and art treasures, which had remained in the Kremlin, were kept here. It was not until the beginning of the 19th century that the Armoury was converted into a museum.

At present it is one of the oldest museums in the Soviet Union, a depository of unique examples of decorative and applied art and culture. All the items in the Armoury are closely associated with the history of the Moscow Kremlin and that of the multinational Russian state.

Among the royal regalia are the famous golden Cap of Monomach, which was used to crown all Russian tsars up to Peter the Great; the first Russian imperial crown of Catherine I, made of gilt silver; the dress of Catherine II adorned with exquisite silver embroidery; and many other precious historical items. The museum also has a display of unique objets d'art in gold, silver, precious stones, ivory, and porcelain, fabrics embroidered with pearls and adorned with precious stones. There is also a very big collection of ceremonial carriages, each one of which is a work of art.

There are special show-cases of gifts to the Russian tsars from foreign ambassadors. The most interesting is the collection of gifts presented by Swedish ambassadors, which includes some 200 valuable items, in particular the rich gifts from Charles XII—rare work by Stockholm craftsmen, brought to Russia in 1699.

The Armoury also contains the world's finest collection of old English silver, made by 16th-17th century London silversmiths.

The Armoury is a treasury of world importance, housing unique works of decorative and applied art. Its collections are evidence of the people's inexhaustible creative genius and artistic talent.

As you leave the Kremlin you will see two more towers crowned with ruby-red stars. The one of the left, by the river, is the **Vodovzvodnaya** (Water) **Tower**, perhaps the most elegant of all the Kremlin towers. It was built in 1485-91; after being wrecked by French troops in 1812 it was finally rebuilt in 1819 to plans by Osip Beauvais. With its star it is around 62 metres high. The other tower is the **Borovitskaya** (it takes its name from the Russian word *bor* meaning forest), through which you may leave the Kremlin. It was erected in 1490 by Pietro Antonio Solari, and consists of three pyramids that become progressively smaller and is topped with an octagonal stone section and nipped roof (tower and star are 54 metres high).

The Borovitskaya Tower is the last stop in our tour of the Kremlin. Three hundred metres from the Borovitsky Gate is Biblioteka imeni Lenina Metro station. You can reach it through an underpass from the Alexandrovsky Gardens, which run parallel to the Kremlin wall.

ALONG GORKY STREET

We suggest you start this walk from the Belorusskaya Metro station. From here you can walk along Gorky Street to the centre and the Kremlin. Gorky Street, one of Moscow's busiest, like many of the other thoroughfares of the city, radiates from the centre. The walk should take about an hour and a half.

Before 1935, when it was given the name of the great proletarian writer Maxim Gorky, this street was called *Tverskaya*. From time immemorial it had led from Moscow to the old Russian town of Tver (now called Kalinin), and on to St. Petersburg, the old capital of Russia. For a long time Gorky Street has been Moscow's main street. Its appearance was greatly altered after its radical reconstruction, begun in 1937. Dozens of the old houses were demolished, while those of value were moved bodily back in the areas adjoining. The street itself was widened from 19 to 56 metres.

As you leave the Metro station you come out onto a square where **Byelorussia Railway Station** is located. Every day trains arrive at this station from Berlin and Warsaw, with carriages from Paris, Vienna, London, Oslo and Stockholm. The station itself is over a hundred years old, and has remained basically the same since its rebuilding in 1909. It is going to be reconstructed and made much larger and more attractive, and the square in front of it will be rebuilt too.

This square and Gorky Street, which seems to flow out of it, have witnessed many warm public welcomes, like the national rejoicing over the successful completion of the Chelyuskin Arctic expedition in 1934, the return from America of the crews of Valery Chkalov and Mikhail Gromov, who made the first non-stop, trans-polar flights from Moscow to the United States in 1937, the homecoming of Ivan Papanin and his team of polar explorers after their now legendary drift on the North Pole ice floe in 1937, and warmest of all, the unforgettable welcoming home in the spring of 1945 of war heroes from the front.

In the centre of the square, in a small garden, is a **monument to Maxim Gorky**, the father of Soviet literature. The statue, designed by Ivan Shadr and made by Vera Mukhina, Nina Zelenskaya, and Zinaida Ivanova, was erected in 1951.

To the left from the Byelorussia Station runs Leningrad Prospekt, a handsome avenue with broad green alleys. And before we begin our stroll down Gorky Street, let me briefly describe the main places of interest along Leningrad Prospekt, since you may see them if you enter the city via Sheremetyevo Airport, or travel to Leningrad by car (725 km) or make an out-of-town excursion to Arkhangelskoye (see pp. 153-154).

The avenue is not only an important transport artery but has large sports facilities, scientific and educational institutions, and industrial enterprises on both sides. On the right-hand side, over the Byelorussia Station viaduct, is the 2nd Moscow Watch Factory, which exports to dozens of countries. Two streets further along is the **Sovetskaya Hotel**, on the site of the once popular *Yar* restaurant. Today variety shows, concerts, and productions of the Romen (Romany) Gipsy Theatre are held in its concert hall. And running to the left is Begovaya Street, leading to the Moscow **Race Course**.

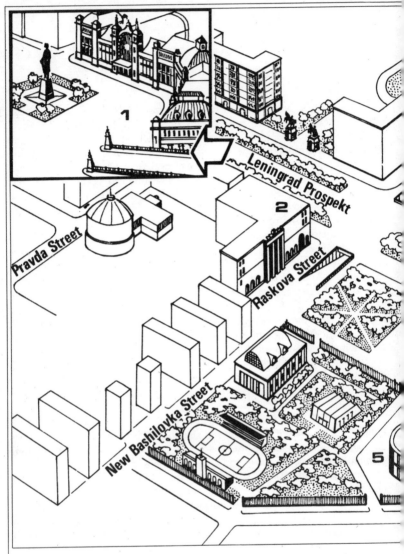

1. Byelorussia Railway Station
2. Sovetskaya Hotel and Concert Hall
3. Race Course
4. Young Pioneers' Stadium
5. Dynamo Stadium
6. Dinamo Metro station

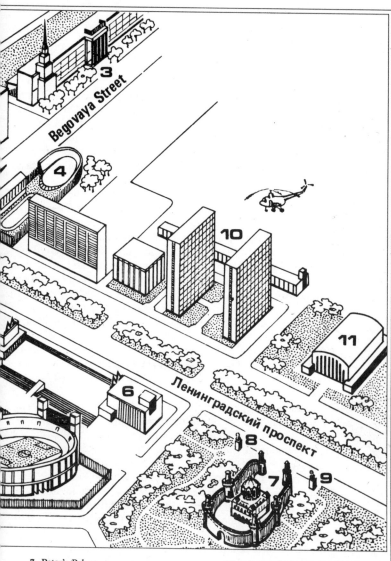

Begovaya Street

Ленинградский проспект

7. Peter's Palace
8. Statue of Nikolai Zhukovsky
9. Monument to Konstantin Tsiolkovsky

10. Air Terminal. Aeroflot Hotel
11. Sports Palace of the Central Army
    Sports Club

A little further along, still on the left-hand side is the **Young Pioneers' Stadium** and the Moscow **Cycle Track.** On the right-hand side, about a kilometre beyond the Sovetskaya Hotel, set in Petrovsky Park, is the **Dynamo Stadium**, a large complex consisting of a sports arena, indoor swimming pool, training grounds, and other sports facilities. For more details on these sports facilities see pp. 137-145.

Almost immediately beyond the stadium is the imposing, graceful, picturesque *Peter's Palace (Petrovsky Dvorets)*. It was built in 1775-82 by the renowned 18th-century Russian architect Matvei Kazakov. Two monuments flank the entrance, one to Nikolai Zhukovsky and the other to Konstantin Tsiolkovsky, both eminent scientists and inventors in the spheres of aviation and astronautics (sculptor Sergei Merkurov).

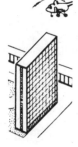

A little further along on the opposite side is the **Moscow Air Terminal**, flanked by two similar twelve-storey buildings, one the **Aeroflot Hotel** and the other the Ministry of Civil Aviation of the USSR. Still further along on the same side is the sports complex of the **Central Army Sports Club,** one of the most popular and successful sports clubs in the country.

Leningrad Prospekt ends beyond Sokol Metro station, at the tall building of the Gidroproekt Institute, where it forks into Volokolamsk Highway and Leningrad Highway.

As you drive along Leningrad Highway *(Leningradskoye Shosse)* look out to the left for the **Northern Port** whose spire rises from a big park on the bank of the Khimki Reservoir. The Port's buildings were designed by Alexei Rukhlyadev and built in 1937. Its cosy Volga Restaurant is situated on the first floor. On the opposite side of the Highway is Friendship *(Druzhba)* Park, which was laid out by the young people taking part in the 6th World Youth Festival in 1957.

But let us now return to the square in front of Byelorussia Station and begin our walk along Gorky Street towards the city centre. Apart from its various sights, Gorky Street has many shops worth visiting. Not far from Byelorussia Station, at 46b on the left-hand side of the street is the exhibition hall of the Artists' Union of the Russian Federation. As we stroll down the right-hand side, we come to The House of Children's Books at No. 43, where young readers' interests are studied, the best children's books advertised and sold, and meetings arranged between children and their favourite authors.

Further along we come to Mayakovsky Square, where Gorky Street crosses Sadovoye Ring, a busy thoroughfare more than 15 kilometres long.

In the centre of the square is a **statue of Vladimir Mayakovsky**, the outstanding Soviet poet, made by Alexander Kibalnikov and unveiled in 1958.

Beyond the monument, at the west end of the square is a tall building with a spire and clock, the **Peking Hotel**, built in 1950. The hotel's restaurant serves Chinese food. At the opposite end of the square, on Gorky Street, is the Sofia Restaurant, which specialises in Bulgarian cuisine. On the corner of the square, diagonally across from the Sofia Restaurant is an imposing building with a portico consisting of ten columns: the **Tchaikovsky Concert Hall**, built in 1940 and seating 1,650. All through the concert season the best Soviet orchestras, choirs, dance companies, musicians and singers, and celebrated foreign artistes perform here. In July and August it is used as **Intourist's Cultural Centre**, where round-table discussions and question-and-answer evenings between foreign tourists and eminent Soviet scientists, statesmen, public figures, and journalists are held. Concerts are given here by national dance ensembles, choirs, and orchestras from the republics of the USSR. The aim of the centre is to help tourists become acquainted with the life and progress of the Soviet Union.

Next to the Tchaikovsky Hall is the **Satire Theatre**, and behind it, in the small, pleasant Aquarium Gardens, is the **Mossoviet Theatre**. Since its formation more than thirty years ago it has been associated with the name of Yuri Zavadsky, an outstanding producer, and pupil of Stanislavsky and Vakhtangov.

Continuing our walk towards the centre we pass a couple of big shops specialising in television and radio sets, and in cameras and photographic equipment and supplies. Across the street from them is the *Malysh* (Toddler) shop, selling toys and clothes for babies and toddlers. Further along, also on the left-hand side, is the **Minsk Hotel** (400 rooms), built in 1964 and well known for its Byelorussian cuisine. Next to the Minsk Hotel, at 22a,

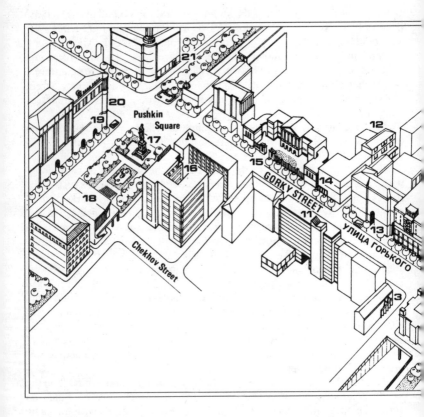

is an old house in which the **Organising Committee for the 1980 Olympic Games** has its headquarters.

On the right-hand side look out for No. 25 Gorky Street, which has a large window display of satirical posters. This is the exhibition hall for one-man shows arranged by the USSR Union of Artists. When you reach Sadovsky Lane, named after the famous dynasty of Russian actors, you will see an eye hospital on the right corner. Its building, designed by Matvei Kazakov in 1780, was moved back from its old site to this position during

1. Byelorussia Railway Station
2. Mayakovsky Square
3. Mayakovskaya Metro station
4. Statue of Vladimir Mayakovsky
5. Peking Hotel
6. Moskva Cinema
7. Sofia Restaurant
8. Tchaikovsky Concert Hall
9. Satire Theatre
10. Mossoviet Theatre. Aquarium Gardens
11. Minsk Hotel
12. Young Spectators' Theatre
13. Radio, cine- and photo-supplies shop
14. Stanislavsky Drama Theatre
15. USSR Museum of the Revolution
16. Pushkinskaya Metro station. *Izvestia* complex
17. Statue of Alexander Pushkin
18. Rossia Cinema
19. Offices of *Moscow News*
20. All-Russia Theatrical Society and Central Actors' Club
21. Armenia Store. Museum of the sculptor Sergei Konenkov

the reconstruction of Gorky Street, and turned through 90° to face this side-street. On the same side-street is the **Young Spectators' Theatre**, where plays for schoolchildren are presented. Crossing the side-street we come to another theatre on Gorky Street, the **Stanislavsky Drama Theatre.** Next to the theatre, at No. 21, is an old mansion with colonnades, set back from the street behind railings, with sculptured lions decorating its gates. It was built in the middle of the 18th century, and restored after the great fire of 1812 by Adam Menelas. Before the Revolution this mansion was the

English Club of the aristocracy. Now it is the *USSR Museum of the Revolution.

The Museum's exhibits trace the path covered by the people of the Soviet Union under the leadership of the Communist Party. The documents and materials displayed describe the initial period of the working-class and revolutionary movement in Russia, the history of the bourgeois-democratic revolutions of 1905 and 1917, and the victory of the Great October Socialist Revolution. An important place is given over to materials on the building of socialism in the USSR, the heroic years of the Great Patriotic War (1941-45) and the building of a developed socialist society. The Museum was opened in 1924, and during its fifty-odd years has been visited by over 40 million people.

This museum has the status of a research institute, and houses more than a million documents, photographs, exhibits, and works of art. Its remarkable collection of paintings, graphics and sculptures is of special interest, as it includes works by the greatest Russian artists of the turn of century—Ilya Repin, Valentin Serov, Sergei Ivanov, Konstantin Savitsky, Sergei Korovin, Vladimir Makovsky, Boris Kustodiyev—and by leading Soviet painters and sculptors—Sergei Konenkov, Boris Ioganson, Isaac Brodsky, Igor Grabar, Konstantin Yuon, Kuzma Petrov-Vodkin, and the Kukryniksy trio. The foreign section of the library contains literature in 34 languages on the history of the international working-class and revolutionary movement. Exhibits include the first Soviet decrees on peace and on land, and "The Declaration of Rights of the Peoples of Russia", adopted by the Soviet Government in November 1917. This document established legislatively the right to free development and complete equality for all the nationalities of Russia, and the right of all nations to self-determination, and abolished all national and religious privileges and restrictions. Documents are also preserved here on the formation of the Union of Soviet Socialist Republics, which was proclaimed on December 30, 1922 at the First All-Union Congress of Soviets. Here, too, is the first Banner of the Central Executive Committee of the USSR, made soon after the Congress, and on which "Workers of All Countries, Unite!" is embroidered in six languages—Russian, Ukrainian, Byelorussian, Georgian, Armenian, and Azerbaijan (the languages of the first republics to join together in the Union of Soviet Socialist Republics). In front of the Museum stands a gun

74

with which the revolutionary soldiers shelled the White Guards in October 1917. Also on exhibit are an old pylon for overhead tram wires which bears scars of the artillery fire during the fighting to establish Soviet power in Moscow, and brought here from Pushkin Square, and a field gun from one of the revolutionary units of the Petrograd garrison. Close by, too, there is an armour plate from the legendary cruiser *Aurora*, whose guns signalled the storming of the Winter Palace in Petrograd.

The Museum of the Revolution is open to the public on Tuesdays and Wednesdays from 12:00 to 20:00, on Fridays from 11:00 to 19:00, and on Thursdays and Sundays from 10:00 to 18:00. Admission is free.

Continuing your walk you come to Pushkin Square, where Gorky Street crosses by Boulevard Ring. On one corner on the left-hand side is the new extension of the offices of *Izvestia*, a daily evening newspaper with a circulation exceeding eight million. An entrance to the new Pushkinskaya Metro station is located here in the building.

In the centre of the Square is the bronze **statue of Alexander Pushkin*, a remarkable work by Alexander Opekushin erected with funds raised by public subscription, and unveiled in 1880. The great poet was very fond of Moscow; he was born here and spent nearly a third of his short life here. These are his verses dedicated to Moscow:

> How oft in grief, from three long parted
> Throughout my vagrant destiny,
> Moscow my thoughts have turned to thee!
> Moscow ... what thoughts in each true-hearted
> Russian come flooding at that word!
> How deep an echo there is heard!

There are always flowers by the pedestal. Just on the eve of the unveiling of Pushkin's statue, the Moscow literary public was honouring Dostoyevsky, and had presented him with a huge laurel wreath. Dostoyevsky, it is said, came to the square and, struggling with the enormous wreath, laid

75

it at the foot of the pedestal, and bowed low to his "great teacher", as he called Pushkin.

Behind the monument, at the end of the square, is the **Rossia Cinema**, built in 1961. Its several halls have a total seating capacity of 3,000. The larger hall has a screen, 14 metres high and 30 metres wide, on which films of every format can be shown. The cinema is also used for international and Soviet film festivals.

Opposite the *Izvestia* building, on the other side of the square, are the offices of *Moscow News*, which appears in different languages, and contains much of interest to the tourist about the city and the Soviet Union.

In the same building, but around on Gorky Street, is the **All-Russia Theatrical Society** and the **Central Actors' Club**, named after the eminent actress Alexandra Yablochkina who was president of the Society for many years. Next to the club is the museum of Nikolai Ostrovsky (1904-36), the distinguished Soviet writer, whose semi-autobiographical novel *How the Steel Was Tempered*, written when he was gravely ill and confined to bed, has been read by generations of Soviet young people and been filmed more than once. Ostrovsky's works have been printed in more than 560 editions in 61 languages of the peoples of the Soviet Union, and in 46 other languages.

On the corner of Gorky Street and Pushkin Square, on the right-hand side of the street, is *Armenia*, a speciality store dealing in Armenian wines, oriental confectionery, and souvenirs. In the same house, on the Tverskoi Boulevard side, is the **Museum of the sculptor Sergei Konenkov** (1874-1971), which was opened in 1974. Everything in the studio is preserved as it was during his life. The collection has 80 of Konenkov's works, including his bust of Lenin, *Cosmos*, and a self-portrait.

 The museum is open daily, except Mondays and Tuesdays, from 11:00 to 19:00.

But let us continue our walk. On the right-hand side are various shops and cafés. Over on the left-hand side, at No. 14, is a very popular Food Store No. 1, built in the early 19th century with big plate-glass windows, a high-ceilinged hall, huge chandeliers, and a sumptuous interior. Further along is a jewellery shop, and next to it the **Tsentralnaya** (Central) **Hotel**, whose restaurant specialises in Russian cuisine. In the same building is a bakery, formerly known as Filippov's. In 1905 its workers came out on strike against the tsarist regime, a strike that was a forerunner of the national strike in October 1905 and the Moscow armed uprising in December of the same year.

Before reaching Sovetskaya (Soviet) Square, on the right-hand side, look in at the **Druzhba** (Friendship) **Bookshop**, which sells books published in other socialist countries.

Facing Sovetskaya Square is the city hall of Moscow, the ***Moscow City Soviet of People's Deputies.** On the high pediment of the Moscow Soviet is the gilt emblem of the Soviet Union.

The banner of the city of Moscow, which is kept in the Moscow Soviet, bears two Orders of Lenin, the Gold Star of a Hero City, and the Order of the October Revolution. The first Order of Lenin was awarded to Moscow on the occasion of its 800th anniversary in 1947. On the 20th anniversary of the victory of the Soviet people in the Great Patriotic War (1941-45) Moscow was declared a Hero City, and awarded a second Order of Lenin and the Gold Star medal, for its outstanding services to the country, and the mass heroism and staunchness of its citizens during the war. And in 1967, on the occasion of the 50th anniversary of the Revolution, the city was awarded the Order of the October Revolution.

The building which now houses the Moscow Soviet was originally a three-storey one, built in 1782 by Matvei Kazakov, and the residence of the Governor-General of Moscow. In 1937-38 it was moved back 14 metres and joined to a new extension. In 1946 it was rebuilt by Dmitry Chechulin, two storeys being added, and the whole portico, with its six pilasters, raised. Over the entrance there is a balcony from which Lenin addressed mass rallies on several occasions. A plaque beside the entrance commemorates these events. Another plaque recalls that in 1917 the building was the headquarters of the Revolutionary Military Council that led the October armed uprising in Moscow.

Since 1924 Lenin's name has been permanently on the roll of deputies of the Moscow Soviet, and after each election the first credentials are made out in his name.

Deputies of the Moscow Soviet, like those of all other Soviets in the USSR, are elected directly by the voters, and are accountable to them. They

1. All-Russia Theatrical Society and Central Actors' Club
2. Nikolai Ostrovsky Museum
3. Food Store No. 1
4. Tsentralnaya Hotel
5. Druzhba Bookshop
6. Moscow City Soviet of People's Deputies
7. Statue of the founder of Moscow, Prince Yuri Dolgoruky
8. Building dating to 1927 by architect S. Chernyshov
9. Statue of Lenin
10. Aragvi Restaurant
11. Moscow Art Theatre

Ogaryov Street

УЛИЦА ГОРЬК

GORKY STREET

exercise their functions without discontinuing their work in industry, schools, or offices. This helps them to keep in touch with the needs and mood of the people, and to respond to the requests and suggestions of their constituencies.

Opposite the Moscow Soviet, on Sovetskaya Square, is an equestrian **statue of Prince Yuri Dolgoruky**, the founder of Moscow, the work of Sergei Orlov, Alexei Antropov, and Nikolai Shtamm. It was unveiled in 1954. Behind it, in a small garden with a fountain, is the building of the **Central Party Archives of the CPSU Central Committee's Institute of Marxism-**

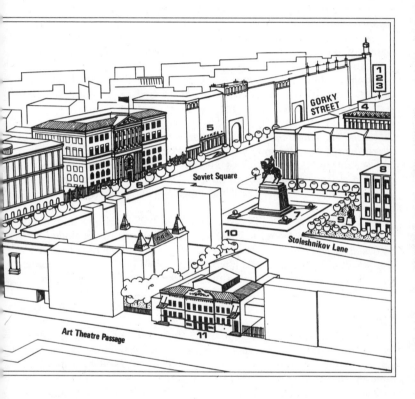

Leninism, built in 1927. The archives contain more than 6,000 manuscripts of Karl Marx and Frederick Engels, and over 30,000 documents of Lenin's. On the building's pediment is a panel with representations of Marx, Engels, and Lenin. In front of the building is a red granite statue of Lenin by Sergei Merkurov, unveiled in 1938.

On the corner of Stoleshnikov Lane, which leads down the hill from Sovetskaya Square, is the famous *Aragvi* Restaurant, which specialises in Georgian cuisine. Stoleshnikov Lane leads to a very popular and busy shopping centre.

As you continue walking along Gorky Street towards the Kremlin, have a look at the two houses (Nos. 9 and 11). At the end of 1941, the nazis who were certain that they would capture the city swiftly, specially ordered some Finnish granite, for a monument in Moscow. After victory over nazi Germany, this granite was used to build the columns of the large archway between these two houses.

Down the hill, on the corner of Ogarev Street is the **Central Telegraph Office** (built by Ilya Rerberg in 1927). In this building are the round-the-clock services of the Central Telephone Exchange.

On the other side of Gorky Street, opposite the Central Telegraph Office, is Art Theatre Passage *(Proyezd Khudozhestvennovo Teatra)*, in which the famous Moscow Art Theatre is located. Its façade is decorated with the theatre's emblem—a seagull. The Art Theatre has two other buildings and stages, one in Moskvin Street at No. 3 (named after a renowned member of the company), and the other, a new building, on Tverskoi Boulevard.

The Moscow Art Theatre was founded in 1898 by Konstantin Stanislavsky and Vladimir Nemirovich-Danchenko. Its repertoire includes plays by Chekhov and Gorky, who were both associated with it in its first years, and Soviet plays including the famous plays about Lenin, *Kremlin Chimes* and *Third Pathetique* by Pogodin and *July 6th* by Shatrov. Gorky said that it was impossible not to love the Art Theatre, which was as much part of Russian and Soviet culture as were the Tretyakov Gallery and St. Basil's Cathedral.

Between the Central Telegraph Office and the Intourist Hotel is another theatre, the **Yermolova Drama Theatre**, named after the distinguished actress Maria Yermolova. Its building, however, is scheduled for demolition, and the theatre will move to new premises, while a hotel that will complete the ensemble of the National and Intourist hotels will be built in its place.

The 22-storey ***Intourist Hotel** was built in 1971. It has 500 rooms (including two-, three-, and four-room suites) and can accommodate 930 guests. Its two restaurants, with their evening entertainments, are very popular.

Our stroll down Gorky Street is almost over. We suggest you now visit the **Podarki** (Gifts) shop opposite the Intourist Hotel. On both corners of Gorky Street you'll find entrances to Prospekt Marxa Metro Station.

SECOND DAY

In the morning we suggest you walk along Marx Prospekt and have a look at the city centre. This will take about an hour and a half; then, before lunch, you will have time to visit the Tretyakov Gallery or the Pushkin Museum of Fine Arts. In the afternoon you might well visit Kalinin Prospekt, one of the new thoroughfares.

ALONG MARX PROSPEKT

Marx Prospekt sweeps in a broad arc north and east through the centre from Dzerzhinsky Square to Bolshoi Kamenny Bridge, across two main squares, Sverdlov Square and 50th Anniversary of the October Revolution Square. It is probably the busiest avenue in the city. The areas adjoining it have many historical and architectural monuments and places associated with the struggle for Soviet power in the city, and with the activity of Lenin. It is around three kilometres long.

We advise you to begin your walk from Ploshchad Revolutsii Metro station, which is connected with Ploshchad Sverdlova and Prospekt Marxa Metro stations by underground passages.

As you come out of the Metro station you will see on your left a three-storey red brick building with a high, pitched roof. Built by architect Dmitry Chichagov in 1892, it was the City Duma (City Hall) of Moscow before the Revolution. In October 1917 counter-revolutionaries barricaded themselves in it to defend the decayed system and the "city fathers". Workers' detachments and revolutionary soldiers, however, took the building after fighting. In memory of these events the square was named Revolution Square.

In 1937 the **Central Lenin Museum**, which was founded in 1924 and contained the country's largest collection of Leniniana, was transferred to this building. It is a major centre of disseminating Lenin's ideas and theoretical heritage; its 34 halls have 12,000 exhibits illustrating his work and life (Lenin's papers and personal belongings, historical Party documents, photographs, printed matter, and works of art). There is also a replica of his study in the Kremlin. The exhibits document Lenin's titanic activity from the 1890s to the very end of his life, from his membership of the first Marxist circles and the creation of the Bolshevik Party in 1903 to struggle for victory of the October Revolution and the formation of the world's first state of workers and peasants. Other exhibits show how, under the leadership of the Communist Party, the Soviet people built socialism and are confidently moving towards communism. The museum contains an impressive collection of Soviet works of art devoted to Lenin: paintings, sculptures, drawings, and works of folk art, including sketches drawn from life and the popular sculptured portraits made by Nikolai Andreyev. There is also the posthumous portrait of Lenin, on which Ivan Shadr worked non-stop for 46 hours during the days of mourning in January 1924, Alexander Gerasimov's painting *Lenin on the Speaker's Stand*, and the canvases of Isaac Brodsky, one of the first artists to portray Lenin, whose recollections of his work on the painting *Lenin at Smolny* are of interest.

> "I single out this painting from my many works devoted to Lenin," Brodsky wrote. "... I wanted to depict Lenin as he really was. But that seemed the most difficult thing.... Every detail in the painting had to be absolutely true. For everything in the room had to be just as it was when Lenin lived in it! The onlooker had to experience the same feeling you get in the museum when you want to touch Lenin's things. ... I made detailed sketches in an album of all the necessary details about the room. The drawing I made at a congress of the Comintern served me as the basis for the image of Lenin."

Interest in Lenin's work and life is unfailing. Since it was opened, the museum has been visited by over 47 million people from 120 countries. In 1977 alone it had over two million visitors, including more than 400,000 from abroad. In 1970 during the centenary of Lenin's birth exhibits were received from 72 countries. For example, letters signed by 1,500,000 people, congratulating the Soviet people on this memorable occasion, arrived from Britain. Many gifts were sent from the socialist countries, and from other countries on every continent.

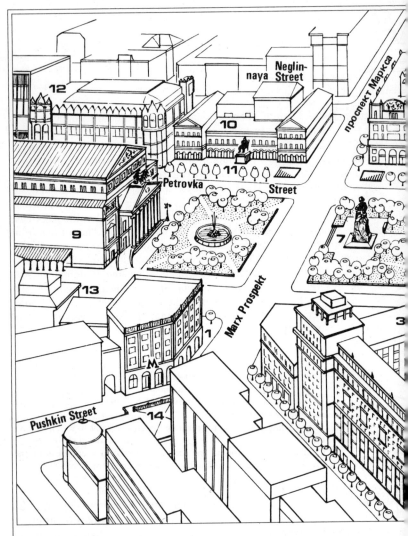

1. Ploshchad Revolutsii Metro station;
   Ploshchad Sverdlova and Prospekt
   Marxa Metro stations
2. Central Lenin Museum
3. Moskva Hotel
4. Walls of 16th-century
   Kitaigorod
5. Metropole Hotel
6. Intourist Central Travel Bureau
7. Statue of Karl Marx

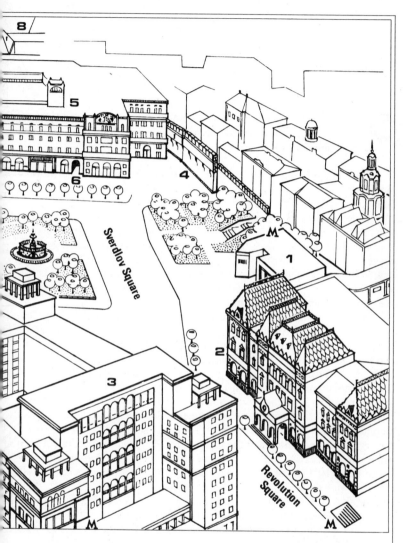

8. Statue of Ivan Fyodorov,
   the first
   Russian printer
9. Bolshoi Theatre
10. Maly Theatre

11. Statue of Alexander Ostrovsky, the
    outstanding Russian playwright
12. Central Department Store (TsUM)
13. Central Chidren's Theatre
14. House of Trade Unions

The Central Lenin Museum is open daily, except Mondays, from 10:00 to 18:00 (on Sundays from 10:00 to 17:00). Admission is free.

Opposite the Lenin Museum is the twelve-storey building of the **Moskva Hotel**, which occupies the whole block between Sverdlov Square and 50th Anniversary of the October Revolution Square.

But let us turn to the right, towards the Metropole Hotel. Just before you reach it, you can see the remains of the old walls of Kitaigorod. Behind it is the **Historical Archives Institute**, whose windows are decorated with carved white-stone surrounds. On its site stood the Royal Printing House, in which Ivan Fyodorov, the first printer in Russia, on April 19, 1563, began and on March 1, 1564 completed the first dated Russian book, *The acts of the Apostles*, now preserved in the Lenin Library.

The ***Metropole Hotel** (which now belongs to Intourist) was built in 1903. In October 1917 the revolutionary workers and soldiers, engaged in fierce fighting to capture it, as some counter-revolutionaries had barricaded themselves inside. There is a plaque commemorating this on the side of the hotel facing Marx Prospekt. Near the entrance to the hotel, on Sverdlov Square, are two other memorial plaques. The inscription on one of them recalls that in the first years after the Revolution the building housed the offices of the All-Russia Central Executive Committee of Soviets of Working People's Deputies, under the chairmanship of Yakov Sverdlov (1885-1919), one of the organisers and builders of the Communist Party and Soviet state. Lenin often made speeches and reports here. To the right of the hotel entrance is the **Intourist Central Travel Bureau**, where you can buy tickets for all types of transport.

The five-storey Metropole Hotel, which has been rebuilt inside several times, was designed by William Walcott. The upper part of the façade is decorated with majolica panels designed by the celebrated artist Mikhail Vrubel (1856-1910) on the theme of the play *La Princesse lointaine* by French playwright Edmond Rostand.

In front of the Metropole, in the public garden among apple trees, roses, lilacs, and tulips is the ***statue of Karl Marx**, designed by Lev Kerbel. Its foundations were laid in 1920 and Lenin spoke at the ceremony. Around it are granite slabs on which are engraved the immortal words: "His name will endure through the ages, and so also will his work! Engels." and "Marxist doctrine is omnipotent because it is true. Lenin." On the plinth is the ardent appeal: "Workers of all countries, unite!"

Let us now cross Marx Prospekt by the underpass and walk towards the Bolshoi Theatre. But if you have time to spare, go up Marx Prospekt (to the right from the Metropole Hotel) and look at the **statue of Ivan Fyodorov**, the first Russian printer, which was sculpted by Sergei Volnukhin and erected by public subscription in 1909. It stands in a small garden on the right of the avenue. Slightly higher up, on the left-hand side, is an enormous department store with large display windows. This is *Detsky Mir* (Children's World), the biggest children's shop in the Soviet Union, built in 1957-64 and designed by Alexei Dushkin. The store has about 500,000 customers every day.

At the end of the street (or rather its beginning, going by the house numbers) is Dzerzhinsky Square with its tall, bronze **statue of Felix Dzerzhinsky** (1877-1926), eminent Party leader, Soviet statesman, and close comrade of Lenin (sculptor Yevgeni Vuchetich).

In the vicinity of this square are three museums that are well worth visiting. The biggest is the **Polytechnical Museum**, whose exhibits, including some unique inventions of gifted craftsmen, trace the development of Russian engineering and show the rapid growth of science and technology in the Soviet years. The others are the **Museum of the History and Reconstruction of Moscow**, and the **Mayakovsky Museum**, the flat where the poet spent the last eleven years of his life.

But let us get back to Sverdlov Square. It is not fortuitous that until 1919 it was called Theatre Square, for two theatres were built here at the beginning of the 19th century. One, a vast, majestic building, was intended for opera and ballet, and the other, a smaller, simpler building, for drama. Ever since the two theatres have been called the *Bolshoi* (Big) and the *Maly* (Little). Both are the national pride of the Soviet people, and everyone visiting Moscow tries to get tickets to them.

The ***Bolshoi Theatre.** The pediment of this majestic building bears four rearing bronze steeds whirling along the chariot of Apollo, the patron of the arts. The work of Pyotr Klodt, they were sculpted over 150 years ago. The Bolshoi Theatre was originally built at the end of 1824 by Alexander Mikhailov and Osip Beauvais. After a fire in 1856 it was rebuilt by

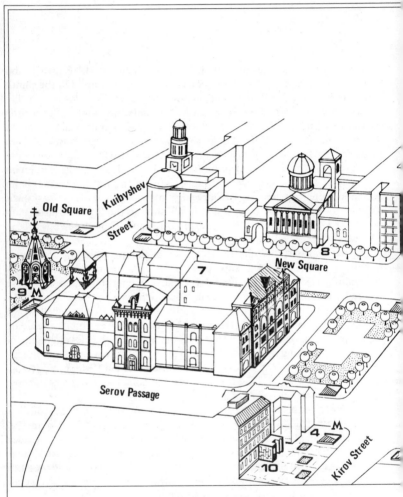

1. Statue of Ivan Fyodorov, the first Russian printer
2. Walls of 16th-century Kitaigorod
3. Slavyansky Bazar Restaurant
4. Dzerzhinskaya Metro station
5. Detsky Mir, the biggest children's shop
6. Statue of Felix Dzerzhinsky
7. Polytechnical Museum

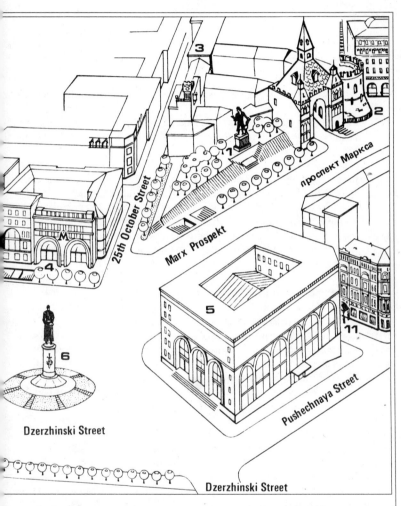

3

2

проспект Маркса

Marx Prospekt

25th October Street

M

4

5

6

11

Dzerzhinski Street

Pushechnaya Street

Dzerzhinski Street

8. Museum of the History and
   Reconstruction of Moscow
9. A memorial chapel to the Russian
   Grenadiers who gave their lives
   in the battle for Plevna in the

Russian-Turkish War of 1877-78.
Ploshchad Nogina
Metro station
10. Mayakovsky Museum
11. Berlin Hotel and Restaurant

Albert Kavos, who made it one of the most handsome theatres in the world.

It was damaged again in a nazi air raid in October 1941, but was completely restored already during the war (in 1943-44). It has five tiers and seats over 2,000 spectators.

Many glorious pages in the history of Russian opera and ballet have been written here. Its performances of works by the founders of Russian classical music—*Ivan Susanin* and *Ruslan and Ludmila* by Mikhail Glinka (1804-57), *Swan Lake, Eugene Onegin,* and *The Queen of Spades* by Tchaikovsky (1840-93)—have been of immense importance in shaping the realistic principles of our vocal and scenic art. The progressive message in its performances of Moussorgsky's (1839-82) *Boris Godunov,* Borodin's (1833-87) *Prince Igor,* and the operas of Rimsky-Korsakov (1844-1908), is vibrant today.

After the victory of Soviet power the Bolshoi Theatre became the premier operatic and ballet theatre of the USSR, famed throughout the world. The works of Russian composers have received a new lease of life on its stage, and its performances of ballets and operas by Soviet composers have been a great success—for example, Prokofiev's *Romeo and Juliet, War and Peace* and *Ivan the Terrible,* Shaporin's *Decembrists,* Asafyev's *Fountain of Bakhchisarai,* Khachaturian's *Spartacus,* and Shchedrin's *Anna Karenina* and *Dead Souls.* Bolshoi also has excellent productions of ballets and operas by famous Western classical composers.

Several Party congresses and All-Union and All-Russia Congresses of Soviets were held in the Bolshoi Theatre, and Lenin often spoke there. It was here at the 5th All-Russia Congress of Soviets in July 1918 that the first Soviet Constitution was adopted. It was also here in December 1920 that the 8th All-Russia Congress of Soviets adopted Lenin's plan for the electrification of Russia (GOELRO). Two years later the 1st All-Union Congress of Soviets proclaimed the formation of the Union of Soviet Socialist Republics. It was here that Lenin spoke in public for the last time, on November 20, 1922. Memorial plaques on the façade of the Bolshoi Theatre commemorate all these events.

The light-yellow building of the **Maly Theatre* was built diagonally across from the Bolshoi Theatre. The **statue of Alexander Ostrovsky**

(1823-86), the outstanding Russian playwright, by the Soviet sculptor Nikolai Andreyev stands at the entrance. The Maly Theatre is often referred to as Ostrovsky House because no fewer than 47 of his plays were staged by it. Like the Bolshoi, the Maly Theatre is the pride of Russian culture, and in October 1974 the whole country celebrated its 150th anniversary. It is credited with having firmly established realism on the Russian stage, and was always closely linked with the liberation movement in Russia.

The plays of Russian classics (Griboyedov, Gogol, Ostrovsky, Lev Tolstoy, and Gorky) and many plays by Soviet and foreign playwrights are performed with invariable success.

The low building of the Maly Theatre stretches from Marx Prospekt to the **Central Department Store** (TsUM), built in 1905 by Roman Klein. In the summer of 1974 a spacious new block was added to the old building. From here along Petrovka and adjoining streets is a big shopping area with a great variety of shops.

Running parallel to Petrovka Street, behind the Maly Theatre and the Central Department Store is Neglinnaya Street. At No. 12 Neglinnaya Street is the **USSR State Bank** and the **Bank of Foreign Trade** (Vneshtorgbank). At No. 8 are the editorial offices of the magazine *Travel to the USSR* published for foreign tourists coming to the Soviet Union. Between Petrovka and Neglinnaya streets runs a cross-street still known as *Kuznetsky Most* (Smith's Bridge), although neither bridge nor smithy has existed for many a year. On Kuznetsky Most are the salons of the **Moscow Artists' Club** (No. 11) and of the **Union of Soviet Artists** (No. 20), a shop selling books in foreign languages, and the All-Union House of Fashions (No. 14).

After looking at the Bolshoi and Maly theatres, and places of interest around them, let us leave the garden in Sverdlov Square in front of the Bolshoi and come out again onto Marx Prospekt. On the corner is Prospekt Marxa Metro station. Next door is another theatre that is quite unique, the **Central Children's Theatre**, founded in 1921, which stages fairy-tales for very young children, and plays for schoolchildren. (There are now, incidentally, 48 professional children's theatres in the USSR, with a repertoire of around 300 plays.)

Let us walk along Marx Prospekt now towards Gorky Street, leaving Sverdlov Square behind us. On the corner of Pushkin Street you will see a low, three-storey building in the Russian classical style, built by Matvei Kazakov in 1784. Before the Revolution it was the Nobles' Club. In 1919 by decision of the Soviet Government it was handed over to the trade unions. Now it is **Dom Soyuzov** (House of Trade Unions). In its Hall of Columns and October Hall important conferences and meetings are held, guests of Moscow honoured, and concerts presented. And at the New Year, parties and entertainments for Moscow schoolchildren are given there.

Lenin often addressed Muscovites here. And it was here, in January 1924, that the mourning country bid farewell to its great leader.

The Moscow public has welcomed many eminent persons in the Hall of Columns. George Bernard Shaw, who had said he did not want to die before seeing the Soviet Union, visited Moscow in 1931. A meeting was held in the Hall of Columns to mark his 75th birthday. Addressing the gathering with the word *tovarishchi* (met with stormy applause) Shaw said he had first learned the word a week before and had grown fond of it.

The site of today's Marx Prospekt was once a maze of narrow, twisting lanes, of *Okhotny Ryad*, an enormous market with butcheries and hundreds of stalls selling meat, fish, game, poultry and greengroceries. The whole thing was demolished during the first reconstruction of Moscow in the 1930s and a broad thoroughfare laid out where the dirty, wooden booths and shacks had been. Two large buildings dominate its central sector: on the left the **Moskva** (Moscow) **Hotel** (its first section built in 1935 and another section added in 1975-76), and on the right the former **building of the USSR Council of Ministers**, built in 1935, which now houses the State Planning Commission. Gorky Street runs off to the right (see pp. 66-80). You must cross it through the pedestrian underpass, coming out at the **National** and **Intourist Hotels.**

In March 1918 Lenin lived for a time in Room 107 on the second floor of the National Hotel, and there is a plaque on the wall commemorating that. The hotel was built in 1903 (architect Alexander Ivanov). In recent years its interior has been completely renovated.

In 1914 H. G. Wells stayed at the National Hotel, and again in 1920 when he returned to have a look at "the country of Bolsheviks" and meet Lenin.

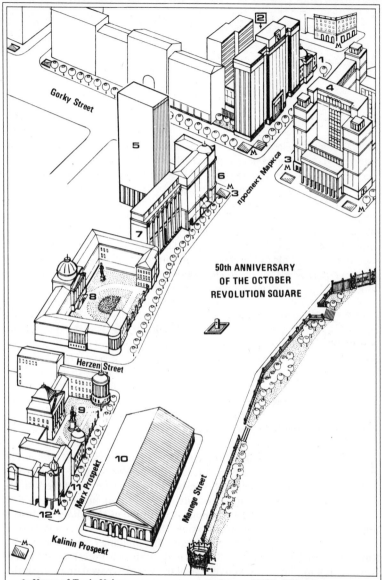

Gorky Street

2

1

M

4

5

M

3

проспект Маркса

6

M

3

7

8

**50th ANNIVERSARY
OF THE OCTOBER
REVOLUTION SQUARE**

Herzen Street

9

10

Marx Prospekt

Manege Street

11

12

M

M

Kalinin Prospekt

1. House of Trade Unions
2. Glinka Music Museum
3. Prospekt Marxa Metro station
4. Moskva Hotel
5. Intourist Hotel
6. National Hotel
7. Intourist House
8. Old building of Moscow
   University

9. Statue of Mikhail Lomonosov
10. Central Exhibition Hall
11. In this building, Mikhail Kalinin,
    head of the supreme body of power
    in the Soviet state, received
    working people.
12. Biblioteka imeni Lenina,
    Arbatskaya, and Kalininskaya
    Metro stations

In 1934 Wells visited Moscow for a third time, and again stayed at the National Hotel. Speaking to reporters, he recalled that in 1920 Lenin said: "Come back and see us in ten years." But Wells "let it run to fourteen ...". Among other things he watched the gymnasts' parade on Red Square. He was stunned, deafened by the vast symphony of colour, the 100,000 smiling young faces. Thus he stood, the writer with an international name, absorbing this new, enigmatic, incomprehensible world. Wells, author of *Russia in the Shadows*, told his Soviet companion that he had come expressly to see these new people of the Soviet Land, and that they impressed him most, more even than the amazing modern industrial achievements of the country, which had been a backward nation before the Revolution.

The imposing seven-storey building next to the National Hotel, put up in 1934 (architect Ivan Zholtovsky), houses the Board of Foreign Tourism of the USSR Council of Ministers and **Intourist**, the USSR Company for Foreign Travel that makes travel arrangements for foreign tourists visiting the USSR and Soviet tourists going abroad. Intourist is one of the world's biggest travel operators. It cooperates with over 700 travel firms and transport companies in almost every country in the world.

Intourist has branch offices and departments in over a hundred Soviet towns and cities. Its 3,500 guide-interpreters help tourists to become acquainted with the country's places of interest, cultural and historical monuments, history, life, and achievements.

From the Intourist building there is a splendid view of the Kremlin. The granite slab one sees in the middle of 50th Anniversary of the October Revolution Square was laid on November 1, 1967, on the eve of the 50th anniversary of the Revolution, as the site of a future monument.

Just beyond the Intourist building is one of the **old buildings of Moscow University**, with two wings overlooking Marx Prospekt. A gently curved dome rises up above its Doric colonnade. The building is characteristic of Russian classicism of the late 18th and early 19th centuries. Part of the university, built in 1786-93 by Matvei Kazakov, was destroyed in the great fire of 1812, during which 6,500 of the 9,000 structures in Moscow were totally or partly destroyed. Moscow had to build afresh. The university building was restored in 1817-19 by the architect Domenico Gilardi, who made a number of alterations to it.

In the courtyard are monuments (the work of Nikolai Andreyev) to two former students—the revolutionary democrats Alexander Herzen and Nikolai Ogarev. Many of the alumni of Moscow University became the pride and glory of Russian and Soviet science and culture.

Crossing Herzen Street, up which, three minutes' walk away, is the **Tchaikovsky Conservatoire**, you will pass another of the old buildings of Moscow University, which received its present appearance in the middle of the last century. In the courtyard of this building there is a statue of the University's founder, Mikhail Lomonosov (1711-65). The statue, made by sculptor Iosif Kozlovsky in 1957, replaces one smashed by a fascist bomb in 1941.

After the vast new University complex was built on the Lenin Hills in 1953, most of the departments were transferred there; but the departments of journalism and law and a few other units remain in the old buildings.

Opposite the old university buildings, on the left of Marx Prospekt, is a long, low massive structure, decorated with friezes in the style of Russian classicism of the early 19th century. This building, formerly the Manège, was built in 1817 by Augustin Betancourt. The wall-to-wall wooden girders hold up its vast roof without intermediate supports. In 1957 the Manège was redecorated and became the *Central **Exhibition Hall**, which accommodates Moscow's largest art exhibitions.

A little further along, Kalinin Prospekt leads off to the right from Marx Prospekt. For many years, people came to talk with Mikhail Kalinin (1875-1946), Chairman of the Supreme Soviet of the USSR, in the reception room in the building on the corner.

There is a beautiful view from this corner of the Troitskaya and Kutafya towers, the Kremlin wall, and the Palace of Congresses.

The whole of the next block, to the end of Marx Prospekt is taken up by the *Lenin Library**. Its main complex was built by Vladimir Shchuko and Vladimir Gelfreikh in 1940. A tall building storing books can be seen behind it. Next to the complex stands the old library building (the former residence of Pashkov, a rich landowner), one of the finest examples of Russian classical architecture of the second half of the 18th century. This house was built in 1786 on a hill opposite the Kremlin by Vassily Bazhenov, and is a typical example of a Moscow town residence of that time. Two wings, supported by four columns, emphasise the vastness of the central section with its main staircase, high portico, and belvedere.

The Lenin Library is the central Soviet public library and is one of the world's largest. It is the state book repository of the USSR, a bibliographical institution covering all fields of knowledge, and a research institute in the fields of bibliography and librarianship. When the library was founded in 1861 it contained over 100,000 volumes, and was then located in the old Pashkov part of the complex. In 1915 its one reading room had a seating capacity of only 170. Lenin worked in it in 1893 and 1897. After the Revolution the library became a major state cultural and educational institution. It now has 23 reading rooms with a total seating capacity of 2,500. The library, with 27 million volumes, daily accommodates around 10,000 people. It actively cooperates in the international book exchange scheme.

14 Central Lenin Museum

15 Lenin Library (old building)

16 Bolshoi Theatre

17 Moscow Art Theatre (new building on Tverskoi Boulevard)

18 The old building of Moscow University. To the left is the Central Exhibition Hall

19 Arbat, one of oldest Moscow's streets

20 Tretyakov Art Gallery, a treasure-house of Russian fine arts

21 One of the typical mansions of old Moscow

22 Pushkin Museum of Fine Arts

23 Kalinin Prospekt. Metelitsa Café, a favourite with young Muscovites

24 Battle of Borodino Panorama Museum. In the foreground is the statue of Field Marshal Kutuzov, commander of the Russian Army in the Patriotic War of 1812

25 Triumphal Arch in Victory Square

26 The building of the Council for Mutual Economic Assistance

19

21

On the left side of Marx Prospekt in a little mansion opposite Metro station is the **Kalinin Museum.** Its exhibits tell of the life and work of Mikhail Kalinin, a peasant's son who became President of the Soviet Union. He was Lenin's comrade-in-arms, an outstanding Party leader and statesman.

When you reach the Lenin Library buildings you will have walked the whole length of Marx Prospekt. We suggest that you then cross over to the Borovitskaya Tower of the Kremlin and walk back through the quiet Alexandrovsky Gardens beside the Kremlin wall to the city centre and Ploshchad Revolutsii Metro station. But if you are tired, you can return to your hotel by Metro from Biblioteka imeni Lenina station.

Alternatively, if you have time, you may continue your excursion and visit either the Tretyakov Gallery or the Pushkin Museum of Fine Arts (which are not far from where you finished your walk along Marx Prospekt). You can get to the Tretyakov Gallery by a "K" bus, which stops near the entrance to the Biblioteka imeni Lenina Metro station (the one nearer Kalinin Prospekt). You get out at the third stop, called Lavrushinsky Lane. For the Pushkin Museum, it is better to walk, for it is only five minutes further along on Volkhonka Street.

The ****Tretyakov Gallery** is at No. 10 Lavrushinsky Lane, a quiet side-street on the other side of the river and the by-pass canal, opposite the Kremlin. It was founded as a city museum in 1892. Its founder, Pavel Tretyakov (1832-98), a Moscow merchant, began collecting the finest works of Russian artists in 1856. Thirty-six years later, in 1892, when he had acquired 1,200 paintings and several hundred sculptures and works of graphic art, he presented the whole collection to the city of Moscow. Today the Tretyakov Gallery has over 7,000 canvases, 5,000 works of early Russian art, over 1,500 sculptures, and 34,000 drawings, water colours, and engravings. Every year the Gallery is visited by over 1.5 million people.

The Tretyakov Gallery is the country's treasure-house of fine arts, and its collection reflects the whole history of Russian and Soviet art.

The collection of early Russian art includes icons by the brilliant artist Andrei Rublev (c. 1360-1430), the outstanding masters Dionisius and Theophanes the Greek (15th century), and Simon Ushakov (17th century). The fine icon *Our Lady of Vladimir* (11th-12th centuries) was brought from Constantinople in the first half of the 12th century.

97

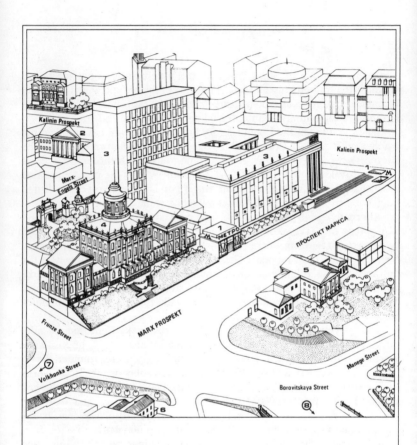

1. Biblioteka imeni Lenina Metro
   station; Kalininskaya and Arbatskaya
   Metro stations
2. Shchusev Museum
   of Architecture
3. Lenin Library (new building)

4. Lenin Library (old building)
5. Kalinin Museum
6. Statue of Mikhail Kalinin
7. To the State Pushkin Museum of
   Fine Arts
8. To the State Tretyakov Gallery

The Gallery has many 18th-century works by Alexei Antropov, Fyodor Rokotov, Dmitry Levitsky, Vladimir Borovikovsky, and others. Russian art of the first half of the 19th century is also well represented, among other things by Orest Kiprensky's portrait of Pushkin, Vassily Tropinin's *Lace-Maker*, Karl Bryullov's *Horsewoman*, Alexander Ivanov's *Apparition of Christ*, to which the artist devoted over 20 years of his life, and sculptures by Fedot Shubin.

Works of the second half of the 19th century are the pride of the Gallery. Of special interest is the work of the *Peredvizhniki* (Itinerants), a school united by democratic ideas and love of the common people, which organised travelling exhibitions (hence its name).

Special rooms are devoted to the work of such outstanding artists as Pavel Fedotov, Ilya Repin, Vassily Surikov, Isaac Levitan, and Nikolai Ghe. There is also an exhibition of the best works of Valentin Serov, Mikhail Vrubel, Nikolai Kasatkin, and Mark Antokolsky, to name only a few.

Soviet art is widely represented in the gallery, which has works by painters, sculptors, and graphic artists like Mikhail Nesterov, Igor Grabar, Konstantin Yon, Isaac Brodsky, Boris Ioganson, Alexander Deineka, Alexander Gerasimov, the Kukryniksy trio, Sergei Konenkov, Vera Mukhina, Nikolai Andreyev, Matvei Manizer, Ivan Shadr, and Sergei Merkurov.

The Tretyakov Gallery's collections clearly reflect the whole, multifarious character and history of Russia, the life, work, and ideals of her people, their struggle for freedom and happiness, and the triumph of the October Revolution.

Lenin visited the Gallery several times after the Revolution, and signed a decree in June 1918 that made it state property of the young Soviet Republic. Since it was nationalised the Government has paid close attention to its needs and has devoted considerable funds to extending its collection and acquiring new works worthy of this unique gallery.

Part of the collection will soon be moved to a new building, which has already been built on Krymskaya Embankment. In the meantime, however, the Tretyakov Gallery remains in its old building on Lavrushinsky Lane. The façade of this building was refaced in 1902 to sketches by Victor

Vasnetsov, which gave it an intricate, bright, fairyland appearance, like a traditional Russian *terem*. The upper section portrays the emblem of old Moscow, St. George slaying the dragon.

The Tretyakov Gallery is open daily, except Mondays, from 10:00 to 20:00 (the box office works until 19:00). Admission 30 kopecks. The nearest Metro station is Novokuznetskaya. As the Gallery is visited daily by around 4,000 people, you would be well advised to book a group excursion in advance, through the service bureau of your hotel. You will then be able to get in without difficulty.

The ****Pushkin Museum of Fine Arts** is at No. 12 Volkhonka Street, one of Moscow's old streets, about five minutes' walk from either Kropotkinskaya or Biblioteka imeni Lenina Metro stations.

Beyond low wrought-iron railings and a line of blue spruces rises its imposing building with a high portico and glass roof. The façade is decorated with twenty-two light-grey granite columns. The building was built in Greek classical style by Roman Klein in 1898-1912 to house a museum of fine arts founded on the initiative of Prof. Ivan Tsvetayev. Since 1937 it has been known as the Pushkin Museum of Fine Arts. It has one of the world's largest collections (in the USSR second only to the Hermitage in Leningrad) of the ancient oriental, classical and Western European art.

The collection has been considerably extended in Soviet times. The additions include many valuable works acquired from other Soviet museums and private collections, and interesting new finds discovered during archaeological expeditions sponsored by the Museum.

The Museum's Egyptian department has one of the world's largest collections of ancient papyruses, objets d'art, bas- and high reliefs, sarcophagi, Fayum portraits, and Coptic fabrics. There are also rich exhibits of the art and culture of Babylon, Assyria, and Persia.

In addition to replicas of all the most famous sculptures of ancient Greece and Rome, there are also original Greek and Etruscan terracottas and vases, and classical sculptures.

The pride of the Museum is its rich collection of Byzantine, Italo-Cretan, and Italian icons.

The picture gallery has over 2,000 works of various schools of painting. Among the masterpieces exhibited are pictures by Italian masters of the Renaissance (Botticelli, Perugino, and Veronese, among others) and fine pictures by artists of the German, English and Spanish schools (15th-19th centuries), and the Dutch and Flemish schools of the 15th-17th centuries (Rembrandt, Rubens, and Van Dyck).

There is a particularly broad and representative collection of French paintings of the 17th-20th centuries, including works by Poussin, Watteau, Boucher, Chardin, David, Delacroix, Corot, and Courbet, an outstanding collection of French Impressionists (Monet, Cezanne, Pissaro, Gaugin, van Gogh, Manet, Matisse, Sisley, Renoir, Degas), and sculptures by Rodin. Among modern works are pictures by Pablo Picasso, by the American artists Rockwell Kent and Anton Refregier, and the Italian Renato Guttuso.

From time to time the Pushkin Museum holds exhibitions of the art of various countries and of individual outstanding artists past and present. Thus, in 1974 there were exhibitions of the Tutankhamen treasures from Egypt, and of Leonardo da Vinci's world-famous *Mona Lisa (La Gioconda)*, and in 1975 of Dresden Gallery collection.

Apart from arranging exhibitions, the Museum carries out extensive research into the world's heritage of art, and maintains contacts with the biggest museums and galleries of the world.

The museum is open daily, except Mondays, from 10:00 to 20:00, and on Sundays from 10:00 to 18:00. It is closed on the last Tuesday of every month. Admission 30 kopecks.

Behind the Pushkin Museum is the **Marx and Engels Museum** at No. 5 Marx and Engels Street. The exhibits include a rich collection of original manuscripts of Marx and Engels, first editions of their works printed in their lifetime, collections of photographs of Marx and Engels and their associates, and works of art devoted to their life and activity. On the wall of one

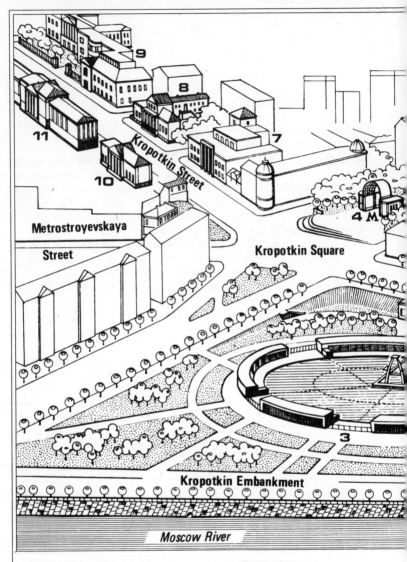

1. Pushkin Museum of Fine Arts
2. Marx and Engels Museum
3. Moskva Swimming Pool
4. Kropotkinskaya Metro station
5. Soviet War Veterans' Committee
6. Central Chess Club of the USSR
7. Soviet Peace Committee, Soviet

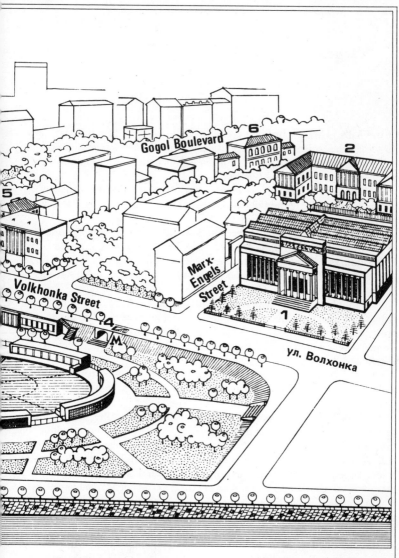

Afro-Asian Solidarity Committee, Slavonic Committee, Soviet Peace Fund
8. Alexander Pushkin Museum

9. Scientists' Club
10. Monument to Frederick Engels
11. USSR Academy of Arts

of the halls is Marx's brilliant prediction: "In contrast to old society, with its economical miseries and its political delirium, a new society is springing up, whose international rule will be *Peace*, because its national rules will be everywhere the same—*Labour!*"

A little further along Volkhonka Street from the Pushkin Museum, on the left-hand side, is the heated open-air Moskva Swimming Pool, which is open all the year round.

Volkhonka Street ends at the junction with Gogol Boulevard (a section of Boulevard Ring already described). At the end of Gogol Boulevard is Kropotkinskaya Metro station. The boulevard runs right to Arbat Square. At No. 4 Gogol Boulevard is the **Soviet War Veterans' Committee** and at No. 14 the **Central Chess Club of the USSR.**

Volkhonka Street is continuous with old Kropotkin Street, which contains some striking examples of old-time architecture that are under state protection. At the mouth of Kropotkin Street a monument to Frederick Engels was unveiled in 1976, by sculptor I. Kozlovsky and architects A. Zavarzin and A. Usachov.

At No. 10, an old mansion, are the offices of many public organisations, including the **Soviet Peace Committee**, the **Soviet Afro-Asian Solidarity Committee**, the **Slavonic Committee**, and the **Soviet Peace Fund.**

In another old mansion, No. 12, is the **Alexander Pushkin Museum**, devoted to the life and literary career of the great poet. Further along, on the same side of the street, is the **Scientists' Club**, which has a popular recital hall. Across the street from it is the **Lev Tolstoy Museum**, which contains a very large collection of various editions of the novelist's works, and much literature on his life and work. And at No. 21 is the **USSR Academy of Arts**, where frequent exhibitions and art shows are held. Kropotkin Street ends at Sadovoye Ring, but the thoroughfare continues as Bolshaya Pirogovskaya Street, at the beginning of which there is a **monument to Lev Tolstoy** unveiled in 1972. A few blocks away is the **Tolstoy Museum**, the mansion where Tolstoy lived and worked from 1882 to 1901, and everything is kept as it was during his life. The street ends by the **Novodevichy Convent**, which has wonderful relics of Russian culture of the 16th and 17th centuries. A little further on, beyond the Moscow Circular Railway is the **Lenin Central Stadium**, a huge sports complex.

ALONG KALININ PROSPEKT

We advise you to begin a walk along the avenue at Arbat Square, using one of the Arbatskaya Metro stations. In the old days on the square stood the Arbat Gates into the city. At this square two important streets, which are commonly known as Old Arbat and New Arbat, diverge. **Arbat Street** is one of the oldest streets, first mentioned in chronicles of early 15th century. Muscovites are very fond of this narrow, winding street with its houses of different heights and styles, and variety of shops. Pleasant side-streets run off from Arbat, where you can find old houses and mansions associated with the names of famous figures in Russian culture. At No. 53 on Arbat itself, Pushkin lived in 1831.

Novy Arbat (New Arbat) is the popular name for a section of Kalinin Prospekt. Work on it began in the spring of 1962, though it had long before been envisaged in the plan for the reconstruction of the city, since Old Arbat was unable to cope with the growing stream of traffic. The avenue, which connects the centre with Kutuzov Prospekt and Minsk Highway by the shortest route, was built on the site of old one- and two-storey, mostly wooden houses, dating from the 19th century.

The plan for the thoroughfare contained a number of original architectural ideas. The architects (Posokhin, Mndoyants, Makarevich, Tkhor, and others) were awarded the Grand Prix of the Paris Architectural Research Centre in 1966 for their modernisation of architectural forms and successful contribution to town planning. In 1963 the new thoroughfare was named Kalinin Prospekt to perpetuate the memory of Mikhail Kalinin, an outstanding leader of the Communist Party and Soviet state.

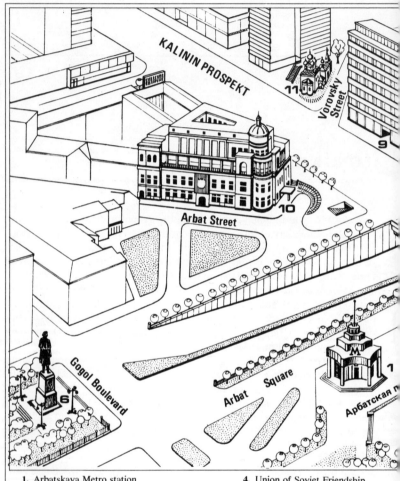

1. Arbatskaya Metro station
   (2 buildings)
2. Khudozhestvenny Cinema
3. Monolith on which it is recorded
   that a "Friendship of the Peoples"
   monument will be erected here

4. Union of Soviet Friendship
   Societies for Cultural
   Relations
   with Foreign Countries
5. Friendship House
6. Statue of Gogol

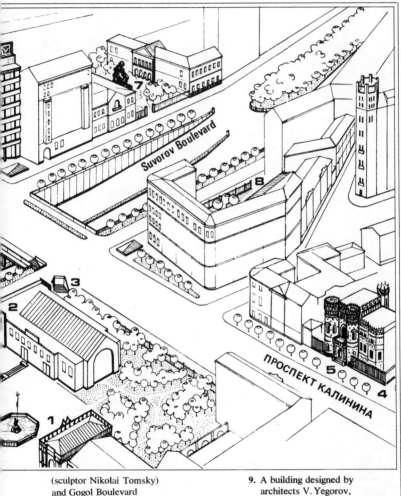

Suvorov Boulevard

ПРОСПЕКТ КАЛИНИНА

(sculptor Nikolai Tomsky)
and Gogol Boulevard
7. House where Gogol lived and the
   monument to the writer (sculptor
   Nikolai Andreyev)
8. Journalists' Club

9. A building designed by
   architects V. Yegorov,
   A. Shaikhet and N. Afanasyeva
10. Prague Restaurant
11. Church of Simon Stylites,
    17th century

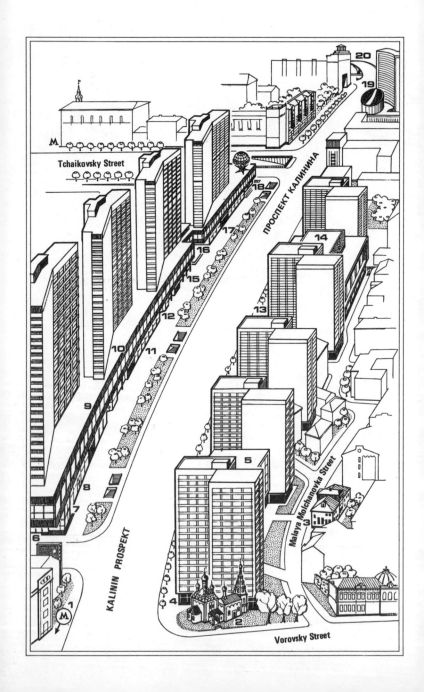

When you come out of Arbatskaya Metro station onto the square, on your right is the Khudozhestvenny Cinema, in front of which you will see a monolith on which it is recorded that here a monument, "Friendship of the Peoples", will be erected.

The choice of the site was not fortuitous, for the **Union of Soviet Friendship Societies for Cultural Relations with Foreign Countries** is located near here at No. 14 Kalinin Prospekt. More than thirty million Soviet people are involved in the activities of the Union and its 64 member societies. The Union works actively in defence of peace and for the promotion of friendship between peoples. Its societies and associations have contacts with 7,000 organisations and many progressive-minded public figures and people in the arts and sciences in 134 countries.

Next to its offices is **Friendship House**, built in 1890s in the style of a Spanish castle. Here meetings are held between foreign visitors and representatives of the Moscow public (factory and office workers, people in the arts, scientists), receptions organised, and concerts, exhibitions, and press conferences take place.

To the right from where we stand, Gogol Boulevard (dipping under Kalinin Prospekt in an underpass) joins with Suvorov Boulevard.

To the left is the **Prague Restaurant**, famous for its Czechoslovak specialities, and across the Prospekt from the restaurant is **Communications House**, built in 1968. This seven-storey building accomodates Moscow's biggest telephone exchange, videotelephone studios, and post and telegraph offices. Not far from it, in a quiet street Malaya Molchanovka, which runs almost parallel to Kalinin Prospekt, is the house (No. 2) where the great poet Mikhail Lermontov lived in 1830-32.

1. Arbatskaya Metro station
2. Church of Simon Stylites, 17th century
3. House where the poet Lermontov lived
4. "Malachite Casket" jeweller's shop
5. The House of Books
6. Zhiguli beer cellar
7. Valdai Café
8. New Arbat Supermarket
9. Moscow Transport Agency
10. Moskvichka fashion shop
11. Charodeika, a major hairdresser's (men and ladies)
12. Jupiter, a large shop dealing in cameras, cine- and photo supplies
13. Melodia record shop
14. Oktyabr Cinema
15. Sintetika department store
16. Metelitsa Café
17. Podarki (Gifts) shop
18. Arbat Restaurant
19. Council for Mutual Economic Assistance, Mir Hotel
20. Kalinin Bridge

A little further on is the small **Church of Simon Stylites**, a lovely monument of 17th-century architecture, which has been carefully preserved and restored. It is now the exhibition hall of the All-Russia Society for the Conservation of Nature.

The church sets off the elegance of the modern 24-storey block of flats nearby. There are five of these blocks on the right-hand side. They were built in 1964-68 and each contains 280 flats.

On the left-hand side of the avenue you see the tall ministry buildings, which are linked by a two-storey, glass-fronted gallery, 850 metres long, with shops, cafés, and restaurants. Kalinin Prospekt has become a favourite walk, as well as shopping centre, for Muscovites.

On the right-hand side near the block of flats whose ground and first floors are taken up by the **Malachite Casket jeweller's shop**, is the **House of Books**, the city's largest bookshop. It is often the meeting place of writers and poets with their readers. The shop deals with literature in all spheres of knowledge. You will find here Soviet publications in foreign languages, including guide-books to Moscow and other reference literature. There is a large stamp-collectors' department in the shop.

The pleasant **Ivushka** (Willow-Tree) **Café** is situated in the next house, and on the other side of the avenue is **Valdai Café**, with a *shashlyk (kebab)* restaurant and wine-bar on the first floor, and the **Zhiguli** beer cellar below (entrance in Arbat Lane).

Next to the **Valdai Café** in the gallery is the huge **New Arbat Supermarket.** Then comes the Moscow Transport Agency and its ticket offices, a florist's and the **Pechora Café**, where young jazz musicians perform in the evenings. The next shop is the **Moskvichka** (Miss Moscow) fashion shop, and after it a big hairdresser's (ladies and men), known as **Charodeika** (Sorceress) and the **Institute of Beauty,** where, it is said, the cosmeticians work wonders.

Next door again is a small photographic studio and **Jupiter**, a large shop dealing in cameras, film, and photographic supplies.

Over on the right of the avenue is the **Melodia record shop**, which sells both classical and folk music, popular songs and albums containing works by Russian, Soviet and other world-famous composers. Next to it is the **Oktyabr** (October) **Cinema**, which seats 3,000. Its façade is decorated by a mosaic of the epic of the October Revolution, made of natural stones (porphyry, granite, jasper and smalt), the work of Nikolai Andronov, Andrei Vasnetsov, and Victor Elkonin. The 2,000 square metres of the mosaic cover the whole of the façade above the ground floor. The building is particularly attractive at night, when the combination of interior lighting and floodlighting creates an impression of transparency, and the cinema seems to glow. In addition to the main hall, there is a small one, seating 500, specialising in short films, documentaries, etc. The foyer can be converted into a large hall for dances, banquets, exhibitions, and concerts. Special equipment makes it possible to show any films, including wide-screen and stereoscopic films.

Next to the cinema is **Seeren** (Lilacs), selling perfumes, eaux de cologne, and cosmetics. After it is a big bakery, which has a wide selection of Russian breads, cakes, pastries and confectionery, with a cosy coffee bar upstairs.

Opposite the Oktyabr Cinema, is an ice-cream parlour-cum-wine bar **Metelitsa** (Snowstorm), very popular with young Muscovites. Next to it are two large shops with departments selling Russian souvenirs, **Sintetika** and **Podarki** (Gifts). And at the end of the block at the corner of Sadovoye Ring is the **Arbat Restaurant** with a floor show. Here too there is a bar, and the Labyrinth Hall in the basement.

From this intersection, where Kalinin Prospekt crosses Sadovoye Ring, there is a good view of the tall building on Smolensk Square that houses the USSR Ministries of Foreign Affairs and of Foreign Trade. It was built in 1951 (architects Gelfreikh and Minkus) and is 172 metres high. Opposite the building are the two high blocks of the **Belgrade Hotel** (each with accomodation for 850).

Kalinin Prospekt continues to the Moskva River and ends with the soaring light building of the **Council for Mutual Economic Assistance** (designers Posokhin, Mndoyants, and Svirsky, and civil engineers Shkolnikov and Ratskevich).

It is the headquarters of the Council's Executive Committee, Secretariat, and various administrative bodies. The Council was founded in 1949 to coordinate the economic development of its socialist member-countries. They are now implementing the Comprehensive Programme for further cooperation and socialist integration including coordination of national economic plans, joint work on scientific and technical problems related to specialisation and cooperation in production, supplies, and marketing. The programme envisages gradual levelling up of the economic development of the member countries—Bulgaria, Cuba, Czechoslovakia, the German Democratic Republic, Hungary, Mongolia, Poland, Romania, the USSR, and Vietnam. Yugoslavia takes part in the work of some of the Council's bodies. Finland, Iraq and Mexico have agreements with it on cooperation in certain fields.

The main 105-metre-high CMEA building is connected with a circular 1,000-seat conference-hall and the 13-storey **Mir Hotel**, which has an attractive bar and restaurant (entrance at Bolshoi Devyatinsky Lane). The architectural ensemble of the Council's buildings makes it one of the most impressive public buildings of the 1960s. Builders of many socialist countries took part in erecting the CMEA complex.

You get a fine view of it from the Ukraine Hotel across the river. You can reach it by crossing Kutuzov Bridge, which is an all-welded metal construction erected in 1957. It is 43 metres wide and with its ramps, around 500 metres long.

From the bridge a good view opens of the beginning of Kutuzov Prospekt, named after Mikhail Kutuzov (1745-1813), the great Russian general, and, on the other bank of the Moskva River, of the recently completed majestic white-stone building of the RSFSR Council of Ministers.

There are two other bridges of interest nearby. One carries the Metro line and the other is Borodino Bridge, so named (as the inscription on it says) "in commemoration of the heroic feat of the Russian people and the glorious Russian Army who defended the independence of Russia in the Patriotic War of 1812".

Kutuzov Prospekt begins with the **Ukraine Hotel**, 172 metres high, a typical example of the architecture of the tall buildings erected in the 1950s. Ornamented with unusual corner turrets, it has a high imposing portico, and a tall spire crowned with a star. It was designed by Arkady Mordvinov. The hotel (1,000 rooms) opened in 1957, and its central section is 20 storeys high.

In the garden in front of the hotel there is a **statue of Taras Shevchenko** (1814-61), the Ukrainian national poet and revolutionary democrat. Unveiled in 1964, it is the work of the Ukrainian sculptors Mikhail Gritsyuk and Anatoly Fuzhenko. The bronze statue stands on a pedestal of Ukrainian granite.

Kutuzov Prospekt runs through an area formerly occupied by run-down housing built before the Revolution, when it was one of the crowded outlying working-class districts of Moscow. The workers' families who once lived in the old houses of this area were rehoused in attractive blocks of flats built by the state.

There are a number of shops of interest to the tourist on both sides of Kutuzov Prospekt. On the Ukraine Hotel side is the House of Toys, the mecca of all Moscow children, which you are well advised to visit if you want to take Russian toys home with you. Opposite it are the **Russian Souvenir** shop (hand-made goods by national craftsmen) and the foreign-currency **Beriozka** shop. We strongly recommend you to visit the **Central Salon of the USSR Art Fund** at No. 6 Ukraine Boulevard, which runs at right angles to the avenue, a hundred metres or so away. There you can find handicraft gifts and works by Soviet artists.

At the forking of Kutuzov Prospekt and Bolshaya Dorogomilovskaya Street rises the impressive **Hero City of Moscow Obelisk**, a granite-clad four-sided prism topped by a gold star, by architects G. Zakharov and Z. Chernyshova, and sculptor A. Shcherbakov.

Here you can stroll at your leisure. Your best way to return to the centre and Arbatskaya Metro station is to take a No. 2 trolleybus or a No. 89 bus.

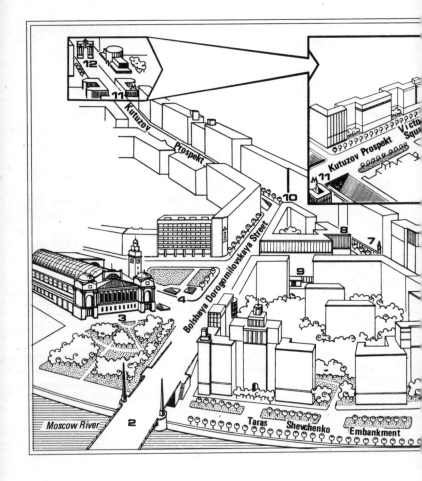

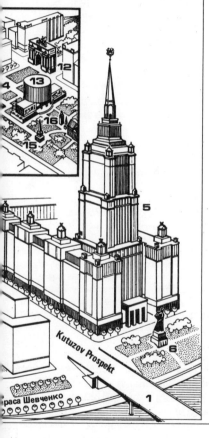

1. Kalinin Bridge
2. Borodino Bridge
3. Kiev Railway Station
4. Kievskaya Metro station
5. Ukraine Hotel
6. The Ukrainian poet Taras Shevchenko
7. The House of Toys
8. Russian Souvenir and Beriozka shops
9. Central Salon of the USSR Art Fund
10. Hero City of Moscow obelisk
11. Kutuzovskaya Metro station
12. Triumphal Arch
13. Battle of Borodino Panorama Museum
14. Statue of Mikhail Kutuzov
15. Obelisk marking the common grave of heroes of the Patriotic war of 1812
16. Kutuzov Hut

But you can also take the same routes and travel to the end of Kutuzov Prospekt, where there are several memorials to the Patriotic War of 1812. Of course, the quickest way to get here is by Metro to Kutuzovskaya station, from where it is either a ten minute walk or two stops on the No. 89 bus or No. 2 trolleybus to the Arch of Triumph at Victory Square, which was so named in 1975 in commemoration of the 30th anniversary of the Soviet people's victory in the Great Patriotic War of 1941-45.

The *Triumphal Arch was erected in 1827-34 in honour of the Russian people's victory in the war of 1812. It was designed by the Russian architect, Osip Beauvais, and formerly stood in front of Byelorussia Railway Station. Later, when Gorky Street was widened, it was taken down and reset on Kutuzov Prospekt in 1968. Originally it was built of brick and faced with white stone. Concrete and steel reinforcing were used when it was re-erected.

> The restored monument is a single arch decorated on all four sides with pairs of Corinthian columns, between which there are statues of warriors and bas-reliefs with allegorical images of different stages of the war. On the top of the arch are female figures representing Courage, Staunchness, and Victory. The arch is topped with the winged figure of Glory in a chariot drawn by six steeds. On one side of the arch there is an inscription taken from orders issued by Kutuzov in 1812; "Brave and victorious troops! ... each one of you is a saviour of your Fatherland! Russia hails you ... Your great feats and deeds will not fade or be forgotten ... Posterity will preserve them in their hearts. You saved your Fatherland with your blood."

Near the Triumphal Arch is another monument to the Patriotic War of 1812, the **Panorama Museum of the Battle of Borodino.** It is a large cylindrical building of glass and aluminium, designed by a group of architects headed by Alexander Korabelnikov, and erected in 1962. The building is more than 40 metres in diameter. Along its walls are 68 cannons captured from Napoleon's army during the Battle of Borodino. The façades of the wings are decorated with coloured mosaics. In front on a high pedestal is a bronze equestrian **statue of Mikhail Kutuzov** by the Soviet sculptor Nikolai Tomsky, unveiled in 1973. On three sides of the pedestal are images of the commanders, soldiers, and partisans who rose in defence of the country. The name of each is given, which lends the whole composition a documentary character.

In the museum there is a remarkable panoramic painting of the Battle of Borodino by the Russian artist Franz Rubo, 115 metres long. Rubo completed his work in 1912 for the centenary of the battle. It was restored in 1949-62 by a group of Soviet artists.

Visitors see the panorama from a six-metre-high observation platform. Between them and the painting is a relief reconstruction of the battlefield 12 metres wide, which gives the impression that they are in the midst of the raging battle that took place on August 26, 1812.

In the courtyard of the museum there is an obelisk marking the common grave of 300 officers and men of the Russian army, heroes of the War of 1812. Not far from the common grave is the museum known as Kutuzov Hut. It was here, in a small peasant's cottage, that on September 1, 1812 at a historic meeting of the Military Council of the Russian Army, Mikhail Kutuzov took the bold and prudent decision to abandon Moscow, but save the army.

The Panorama Museum of the Battle of Borodino is open daily, except Fridays, from 10:30 to 19:00 (in summer from 9:30 to 20:00). It is closed on the last Thursday of every month. Admission 20 kopecks.

THIRD DAY

You have now been in Moscow for two days and have been able to see something of how Muscovites live, to visit many places of interest, and to admire the sights. To broaden your acquaintance with the city and get a general idea of the USSR, we suggest you visit the USSR Economic Exhibition (or VDNKh—Russian abbreviation of the name).

The Exhibition grounds are a huge park, with quiet ponds and blue lakes, gardens and birch groves, shady summerhouses, cafés, and restaurants, and a fun fair. It is a very pleasant place to rest.

We would advise you to visit the Economic Exhibition, which is situated near VDNKh Metro station, during the first half of the day, and after lunch go for a stroll round the Lenin Hills (Leninskiye Gory Metro station).

AT THE USSR ECONOMIC ACHIEVEMENTS EXHIBITION

The Exhibition grounds cover an area of 216 hectares at the end of **Mir** (Peace) **Prospekt**, one of the radial thoroughfares passing into Yaroslavl Highway. The Economic Exhibition was opened in 1959 on the site of the former Agricultural Exhibition, and functions all year round. It has 100,000 exhibits, frequently renewed, that give the visitor a comprehensive picture of the present level and latest achievements of Soviet industry, agriculture, building, transport, science, and culture. It is also a kind of school of advanced work. (The building section, please note, is on the other side of Moscow, at No. 30 Frunze Embankment, not far from Frunzenskaya Metro station. Its exhibits and displays trace the development of construction in the USSR, including housing construction, its methods, the machinery used, and future plans.)

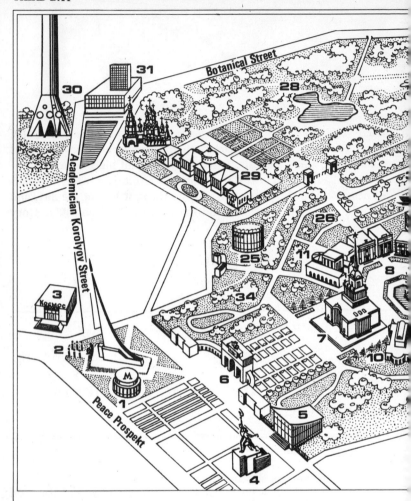

1. VDNKh Metro station
2. Space Obelisk. Alley of Heroes. Statue of Tsiolkovsky
3. Cosmos Cinema
4. The sculpture "Worker and Collective-Farm Woman"
5. Pavilion brought to Moscow from the 1967 Montreal World Fair
6. Main entrance to the Economic Exhibition
7. Central Pavilion
8. The Friendship of the Peoples fountain
9. The Stone Flower fountain
10. Atomic Energy Pavilion
11. Public Education Pavilion
12. Mechanisation and Electrification of Agriculture Pavilion
13. Metallurgy Pavilion
14. Health Pavilion
15. Culture Pavilion
16. Agriculture Pavilion

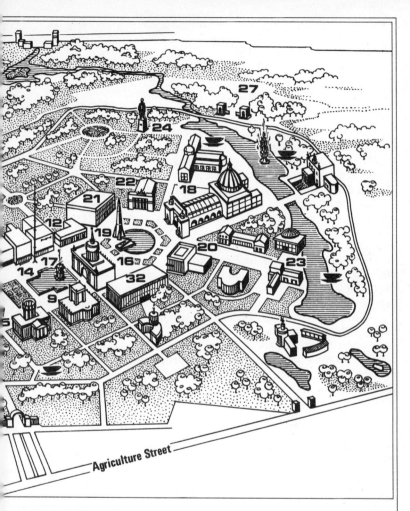

17. Radio-Electronics Pavilion
18. Cosmos Pavilion
19. Vostok space rocket
20. Electrification Pavilion
21. Chemical Industry Pavilion
22. Transport Pavilion
23. Animal Husbandry Pavilion.
    Demonstration Ground
24. Michurin Orchard
25. Circorama
26. Yarmarka (the shopping centre).

Restaurants and cafés
27. Main Botanical Gardens
28. Dzerzhinsky Park
29. Ostankino Museum of Serf Art
30. TV Tower; Seventh Heaven
    Restaurant
31. Television Centre and Olympic TV
    and Radio Complex
32. Temporary Exhibits Pavilion
33. Open-air theatre
34. Fun Fair

The Exhibition has around 300 buildings and 80 pavilions with open-air displays. It takes a long time to walk round the whole grounds, but there is a frequent service of sightseeing trains that make a tour of them in 30 minutes, picking passengers up at various stations and dropping them at others. The fare for the round trip is ten kopecks.

The Exhibition is always seething with life. In all the pavilions there are various temporary exhibits of an educational type mounted for specialists. Here visitors regularly meet the leading people in industry, scientists, journalists, writers, artists, and foreign guests.

The best way to reach the Exhibition is by Metro to VDNKh station. When you come out of the station, turn left and you will see the **Space Obelisk**, a silvery shaft soaring in a curve to a height of 96 metres. It was designed by architects Mikhail Barshch and Alexander Kolchin, and sculptor Andrei Faidysh-Krandiyevsky, to commemorate the Soviet breakthrough into space. It was unveiled in 1964. The main shaft consists of a steel frame faced with sheets of polished titanium. On both sides of its granite base are sculptures depicting the people who made the first manned space flight possible and those who today are boldly continuing space exploration.

In front of the obelisk is a **statue of Konstantin Tsiolkovsky**, the scientist and inventor who not only predicted manned space flights but also created the theory of modern rocketry and astronautics.

Between the obelisk and Mir Prospekt is the **Alley of Heroes**, a walk lined with bronze busts of Soviet cosmonauts, Yuri Gagarin, Valentina Nikolayeva-Tereshkova, Pavel Belyayev, Alexei Leonov, and Vladimir Komarov. At the end of the Alley is a **monument to Sergei Korolyov**, the designer of the first Soviet rockets and spaceships.

To the left of the monument is a widescreen cinema, **Cosmos,** seating 1,600.

From the square in front of the Space Obelisk you get a good view of the main entrance to the Exhibition grounds and the Central Pavilion's 35-metre spire with a golden star. Looking slightly to the right you will see, about 500 metres away, the stainless steel sculpture **Worker and Collective-Farm Woman**, made by Vera Mukhina for the Soviet Pavilion at the 1937 Paris World Fair. This unique work of monumental art has become a symbol of the Soviet Union for many people throughout the world. It is about 25 metres high and weighs 75 tons.

Just behind the monument rises the largest structure in the Exhibition. It was originally the USSR Pavilion at the 1967 Montreal World Fair. After the Fair was over, it was dismantled, brought to Moscow and re-erected here.

The Exhibition is arranged according to branches of the economy, science, and culture. Thus the visitor to a pavilion can get a picture of one particular branch of industry, agriculture, or science on a country-wide scale. The original architecture of the pavilions reflects the national art traditions of the various Union republics.

When you pass through the main entrance a broad walk with fountains and a double row of lamp standards in the shape of ears of wheat leads to the **Central Pavilion**, where the Exhibition proper begins.

In front of the pavilion there is a statue of Lenin. Above the entrance are the state emblems of the 15 Union Republics, and above them the Emblem of the USSR. The exhibits in the Central Pavilion deal with the major social, political, economic, and cultural achievements of the Soviet people. In its five halls are illuminated charts, documents, and works of art on the historical significance of the Great October Socialist Revolution and the Soviet people's efforts to build the first socialist state in the world. As you enter, you see two large paintings by Pavel Sokolov-Skalya, *The Storming of the Winter Palace* and *Lenin Proclaims Soviet Power at the 2nd All-Russia Congress of Soviets.*

A huge illuminated map of the Soviet Union in the main hall reflects the development of key industries. The exhibits in the other halls illustrate the steady growth in the real income of Soviet people and their rising standard of living.

Beyond the Central Pavilion is a vast expanse of Friendship of the Peoples Square, with two fountains—Friendship of the Peoples and The Stone Flower. The thousand jets of the Stone Flower fountain spray water to a height of 20 metres. It is particularly attractive at night when its lit-up stones sparkle in a fairy-like emerald cascade of water.

Friendship of the Peoples Square is surrounded by several pavilions. The first on the right is the **Atomic Energy Pavilion.** A central place in it is occupied by a scale model of the biggest Soviet proton synchrotron—the accelerator at Serpukhov. The pioneering role of Soviet scientists in peaceful uses of atomic energy is also graphically demonstrated by scale models of an atomic power station, of installations for the direct conversion of nuclear energy into electricity, and an atomic-powered ice-breaker. Of special interest is the Rokus apparatus for combating cancer. Also on display are numerous radio-isotope instruments widely used in science, engineering, and medicine.

To the left of the Central Pavilion is the **Public Education Pavilion**, showing the enormous strides made in this field in the Soviet Union where illiteracy has been completely wiped out.

Next come three pavilions of the USSR Academy of Sciences—**Biology**, **Physics**, and **Chemistry**—devoted to the work of our scientists, particularly in the fields of solid state physics, semi-conductors, quantum radio-electronics, cybernetics, the chemistry of organic elemental compounds, radiation chemistry, and the biology of the living cell.

Developments in the Soviet iron and steel industry are broadly demonstrated in the **Metallurgy Pavilion.** On display, for instance, is a scale model of a 2,700 cubic metre blast furnace that was blown in at the Krivoi Rog Iron and Steel Works in the Ukraine and produces nearly two million tons of pig iron a year, which is just half the total output of the Russian steel industry before World War I.

Along the central walk is a small greenhouse with a display of the subtropical plants grown in the USSR, including tea, oranges, tangerines, lemons, olives, laurel, and bamboo. Beyond the greenhouse is the **Health Pavilion** and opposite it the **Culture Pavilion** with an exhibition hall in which works by artists from the fifteen Soviet Republics are displayed. This pavilion also has interesting theatre, cinema, and circus exhibits.

Beyond the Stone Flower fountain is a building the colour of wheat. This is the **Agriculture Pavilion.** Its exhibits tell the story of how Lenin's plan for cooperation in farming was implemented, and show the social, economic, and cultural changes that have taken place in rural life. That is also the theme of the **Mechanisation and Electrification of Agriculture Pavilion**, which is to the left of the main walk leading from the Stone Flower to Industry Square.

On the same side of this walk are the **Computer, Radio-Electronics**, and **Electrical Engineering** pavilions. We recommend a visit to the last-named. Its many exhibits include electric-drive wheels for heavy-duty motor vehicles, tractors, and trailers. Vehicles with wheels of this type are the future of heavy-duty road transport. This pavilion also contains exhibits of household appliances, models of the latest refrigerators, electric and immersion heaters, to name but a few. The exhibits of consumer goods are a good illustration of how the plans of the Communist Party to improve the people's standard of living are being implemented.

On Industry Square is the large **Cosmos Pavilion.** In front of it is a carrier rocket like the one that put Yuri Gagarin in orbit in the Vostok spacecraft on April 12, 1961.

The exhibition prepared by the USSR Academy of Sciences and a number of industrial enterprises demonstrates the Soviet Union's progress in rocketry and space navigation. On display are the world's first artificial satellites, space rockets, Vostok, Voskhod, and Soyuz spacecraft, and the Salyut orbital research station. The first Sputnik, launched on October 4, 1957, which opened the space age in man's history, weighed only 83.6 kilograms. The Proton space probe weighed 12.2 tons, and required a carrier rocket with a total thrust of more than 60 million h.p., three times the power of the rocket standing outside the pavilion.

The exhibits include the recovery capsule, orbital compartment and ejection seat of the Soyuz spaceship; the cosmonaut's outfit; control instruments; geophysical rockets that can lift a payload of 1.5 tons of apparatus to a height of 500 kilometres, and exact replicas of Soviet *lunniks*, the first automatic probes and interplanetary stations sent on flights lasting many months to Mars and Venus, and of the Lunokhod-2 car placed on the surface of the Moon by the Luna-21 probe in January 1973.

There are unique exhibits and photographs illustrating the flights of Soviet cosmonauts, including Yuri Gagarin, Valentina Nikolayeva-Tereshkova, the world's first woman cosmonaut, and Alexei Leonov, who pioneered space walks. A special exposition is devoted to the flights of the Soyuz-4 and Soyuz-5 spaceships, and their docking and transfer modules. The Soviet programme of space cooperation with the socialist countries, as well as with France, India, and the USA is illustrated. Of great interest are the exhibits devoted to the historic joint flight of Soviet and American spacecraft, Soyuz and Apollo, in July 1975, which resulted from the desire of the peoples of the Soviet Union and the USA for peaceful cooperation and detente. The exhibits in the pavilion tell of the docking of these craft in space, and of the extensive programme for scientific and technical research carried out by the Soviet cosmonauts Alexei Leonov and Valery Kubasov and the American astronauts Thomas Stafford, Donald Slayton and Vance Brand.

The **Electrification, Chemical Industry** and **Transport** pavilions are also of interest. The last-named has a life-size test model of an electromobile for carrying freight and mail, which will help combat air pollution in cities. If you go into the Electrification pavilion, have a look at the large map of the USSR showing the network of power stations built in Soviet times.

The large pavilion to the right of Industry Square contains a display of consumer goods. Various foreign exhibitions are periodically arranged there.

Two passenger aircraft are on display in Industry Square, a YaK-40, designed for local flights, and a TU-134 jet airliner, designed for short and medium-length flights. These aircraft are in wide use in the USSR and have been bought by airline companies abroad.

If you walk to the right from Industry Square you will come to the **Animal Husbandry Pavilion** and its show ring. By taking the walk going left from it you will come to the Michurin Orchard, so called because it is mainly planted with the best varieties of hard and soft fruits developed by the renowned Soviet plant breeder Ivan Michurin (1855-1935).

There are many more pavilions, displays, and places of interest in the Exhibition, but it would take at least a week to visit them all. That explains why we have singled out only a few.

The Exhibition also has various entertainments. There is an open-air theatre seating 3,400, where professional and amateur companies perform (dance ensembles, choirs, and symphony orchestras). There is also a variety theatre, a fun fair (with roundabouts, Russian swings, rockets, bumper cars, etc.), a small zoo, and a **Circorama**, a cinema with no seats, where you stand in the middle of a round hall with a great screen all round you. The effect is exhilarating. Shows last 20 minutes (admission is 30 kopecks). The Circorama and fun fair are near the main entrance.

At the Exhibition you can sample the national dishes of many of the peoples of the USSR. They are served at the various restaurants—*Zolotoi Kolos* (Golden Sheaf), *Okean*, (Ocean), *Podkova* (Horseshoe), and *Leto* (Summer)—and *shashlyk* grills—*Baku, Otdykh* (Rest), *Vostochnaya* (Eastern) and *Yuzhnaya* (Southern).

Angling is permitted in the many ponds of the Exhibition (fishing gear can be hired from a booth on the bank). And there is a boating pond. Or you can just sit and watch the swans (black and white), and the wild ducks and geese.

In winter many walks are flooded and converted into skating rinks, where people come to skate to the strains of lively music. And during the annual *Russian Winter Festival* (December 25 to January 15) there are rides in real Russian troikas. There is also a shopping centre **(Yarmarka)** which sells the most varied kinds of goods.

The Exhibition is open all year round daily from 10:00 to 22:00, and at the weekend from 10:00 to 23:00. Pavilions are open from 10:00 to 19:00. Admission 30 kopecks for adults and ten kopecks for children.

The Exhibition gardens adjoin the **Main Botanical Gardens** of the USSR Academy of Sciences in the north and **Dzerzhinsky Park** in the west. The best way to get to the Botanical Gardens is to go through the grounds of the Exhibition to the Khovansky Gate, near the shopping centre. The Botanical Gardens are then immediately on your right, and Dzerzhinsky Park straight ahead.

The Botanical Gardens cover an area of 361 hectares. Their shady oak woods, birch groves, and rose gardens (which contain 16,000 rose bushes of many varieties) attract many visitors. The Gardens have a unique collection of hundreds upon hundreds of the world's rarest plants. It is also a centre for botanical research.

In Dzerzhinsky Park is the renowned *Ostankino Palace,  a beautiful specimen of Russian architecture and decorative art. It belonged to the family of the Counts Sheremetyev, and was built in 1792-97 by serf architects under Pavel Argunov, also a serf.

The structure is built completely of wood in the Russian classical style. The façade facing the entrance to its grounds has a portico topped by a rotunda. The façade facing the garden has a portico with ten columns.

The interior of the Palace—foyer, state rooms, and galleries—is lavishly decorated. The exquisite wood carving of the furniture, doors, and walls, the skilfully laid parquet of valuable kinds of wood, the cut-glass and bronze chandeliers, and the rich collection of carved gilt standard lamps and ash-stands were all the work of serf craftsmen. The paintings, especially those by the Argunovs, who were serf artists, and the rich collections of porcelain, pictures, prints, and sculptures are also of interest.

The whole central section of the Palace is a theatre, one of the finest in Russia of its time. The players were all serf actors and actresses. One of them, the talented actress Praskovya Zhemchugova, was particularly renowned.

In 1917 the Ostankino estate was nationalised and became a museum of the work of serf craftsmen. Concerts of early Russian music are frequently held there.

Next to the Palace is the five-domed Trinity Church, an interesting example of late 17th-century Russian architecture.

In 1967 a new Moscow landmark rose in Ostankino, the concrete **TV Tower,** one of the world's tallest structures, 533 metres high, and 50 metres in diameter at the base. At the 337 metre level there is an observation platform, which is also the foyer for the Seventh Heaven Restaurant, whose three dining halls seat 288 guests. Their floors slowly rotate one full revolution in 40 minutes

27 USSR Economic Exhibition. View of the Central Pavilion

28 Cosmos Pavilion. The interior

29 At the USSR Economic Exhibition

30 Main entrance to the Economic Exhibition

31 Sculpture "Worker and Collective-Farm Woman" by Vera Mukhina before the Economic Exhibition

32 Space Obelisk commemorating Soviet outer space breakthroughs. In front of it is a statue of Tsiolkovsky

33 Lenin Central Stadium. View from Lenin Hills

34 Lomonosov Moscow University. (The new building on Lenin Hills)

35 Vernadsky Prospekt. In the foreground is the new Moscow Circus

36 Metro bridge over Moskva River

37 Lenin Prospekt

38 Palace of Sports at Luzhniki

39 TV Tower in Ostankino

27

34

or so, so that the diner sees a panorama of Moscow during the meal. The view from both observation tower and restaurant on a clear evening is marvellous.

Near the TV Tower is the huge Television Centre, with studios, concert hall, and offices. Its programmes, sent out from the Tower, cover a radius of 150 kilometres obviating relay stations. The TV Centre is linked through Intervision and Eurovision with all countries in Europe, and through communications satellites with almost all points on the Earth's surface.

Our sketch of this interesting area of Moscow is about completed. We suggest that you visit the observation platform and the Seventh Heaven Restaurant. You can book tickets for the Tower and a table through the service bureau of your hotel or at Intourist's Central Excursion Bureau (1 Gorky Street).

THE LENIN HILLS

Before you leave Moscow we suggest you spend a little time out on the **Lenin Hills** (*Leninskiye Gory*), a favourite spot with Muscovites with a fine view of Moscow that they always like to show their guests.

The Hills have an interesting history. They used to be called Vorobyovy Hills after the village that was once here. In 1826 young Alexander Herzen and Nikolai Ogarev, the progressive thinkers and leading revolutionary democrats of their time, swore a solemn oath here to devote their lives to struggle for the people's freedom.

In the years before the Revolution workers gathered here for secret political meetings and May Day rallies. And from here, in October 1917, revolutionary soldiers shelled the counter-revolutionaries.

1. Leninskiye Gory Metro station and Metro bridge
2. Glass-enclosed escalator
3. Moscow Palace of Young Pioneers
4. Moscow Circus (new building)
5. Universitet Metro station
6. Lomonosov Moscow University (new building)
7. Observation platform
8. To the Olympic village

There is probably no better place for taking in all Moscow at a glance. The easiest way to get there is by taxi or with an Intourist excursion. The whole trip will then not take more than an hour and a half. But you can also go on your own by Metro to Leninskiye Gory station.

This station is unlike any other in the Metro's system. It crosses the Moskva River by a two-level reinforced concrete bridge. The upper level is for vehicles, and the lower is the Metro station enclosed in glass, and there are pedestrian walks on each side. The main span of the bridge is about 200 metres long. The bridge connects the residential district of Komsomol Prospekt with that of Vernadsky Prospekt, most of which was built in the last fifteen to twenty years.

When you get out of the train, walk in the same direction as the train. This will bring you out on the right bank of the Moskva River. About 50 metres away there is a glass-enclosed escalator that takes you to the top of the hill. As you go up you will get a beautiful view over the Moskva River and the city.

The river incidentally is 115 metres above sea level, and the top of the hill is 85 metres above the river.

When you get off the escalator you come out on Vorobyovskoye Highway. The shady avenue to the right leads to an observation platform fifteen or twenty minutes' walk away. But let us say first a few words about the two buildings you can see on the other side of Vorobyovskoye Highway, up on the left side of Vernadsky Prospekt—the Palace of Young Pioneers and the new Circus.

The **Moscow Palace of Young Pioneers** (named after the 40th Anniversary of the All-Union Pioneer Organisation), sometimes called Pioneerland, was opened in June 1962. It is a large club and recreation and play centre for schoolchildren. Near the entrance is a statue of metal and stone of Malchish-Kibalchish, a character in Arkady Gaidar's *Military Secret*, a favourite book of Soviet boys and girls. In the expanse of its lawn, criss-crossed with flagged paths, is the Parade Ground, where the crimson flag of the Pioneers flutters from

a tall flagstaff. Here various ceremonial rallies of the Pioneer organisation are held; on festive occasions a Pioneer campfire burns in a great bowl there. The Parade Ground is the centre of the whole architectural complex of Pioneerland. The main building is a two-storey palace, with glass walls and a bright panel of coloured tiles and smalt. The walls of the Palace are decorated with artistic compositions in coloured brick on the theme of Man's conquest of Nature on land, sea, and air. There are 400 rooms where younger children can play games, sing and dance, and rooms for schoolchildren, a Museum of Pioneer Glory, the Lenin Hall where children are ceremonially admitted into the Young Pioneers organisation, and the Club of Fascinating Knowledge.

Adjoining the main building are blocks with well-equipped laboratories, workshops, rooms for making various models, studios and rooms for young painters, sketchers, amateur film makers, elocutionists, actors, musicians, and dancers, cooks, and would-be motorists. All these facilities are always busy.

The Palace has its own concert hall and theatre, its own sports stadium and gymnasiums, an artificial lake for learning to sail, row, and canoe, and a large tract for young naturalists, agronomists, bee-keepers, and gardeners.

Experienced teachers and activity leaders see to it that children get every opportunity from early childhood to develop their gifts and talents. In addition to this Palace, there are 36 district Young Pioneer Houses in Moscow. The upkeep of them all, and the payment of those who run the studios and activity groups, are borne by the state and the trade unions.

Along past the Palace of Young Pioneers, near Universitet Metro station, on Vernadsky Prospekt, is the new ***Moscow Circus,** opened in the spring of 1971 (architect Yakov Belopolsky). This building, which seats 3,400, has a ring with four interchangeable floors that can be switched for one another in a matter of five minutes. One is an ordinary circus ring, another is a pool for aquatic shows, a third a rink for ice ballet, and the fourth, a special ring for magicians. Two foyers, with buffets, encircle the arena on two levels. Animals taking part in the performances are housed in a "hostel" with exercise pens and a kitchen.

Muscovites are very fond of the circus, and Soviet circus is famous all over the world. For example, everyone knows the Soviet clowns, Oleg Popov and Yuri Nikulin, the lion-tamer, Irina Bugrimova, and Valentin Filatov's bear circus. There is another circus in the centre, on *Tsvetnoi Boulevard* (the old circus), and in summer there is often a traditional circus in a tent in Gorky Park (on *Krymsky Val*) and in Izmailovo Park. They are a good idea for an evening outing. Tickets can be booked through the Service Bureau in your hotel.

Fairly near the new circus and almost parallel with Vernadsky Prospekt is Lenin Prospekt, one of the longest avenues in the city. Most of it was built in the last 20 years on the site of villages, meadows and ravines.

Lenin Prospekt begins at October Square *(Oktyabrskaya Ploshchad)*. There is a Metro station of the same name there. The avenue ends at the Moscow Circular Road. Along it are dozens of higher educational establishments and research institutes, the USSR Academy of Sciences, and the headquarters of the All-Union Central Council of Trade Unions (at No. 42) and Sputnik Hotel (at No. 38).

Lenin Prospekt is a busy shopping street, with the *Moskva* department store, *Shoe House, Porcelain House, Fabrics House, A Thousand Odds-and-Ends, Spring* and *Topaz,* and three shops specialising in goods from Bulgaria *(Varna),* Czechoslovakia *(Vlasta).*

At the very end of the avenue is the complex of the Central Tourist House, including a hotel, the Tourist Shop, and sports facilities. Opposite them is the campus of **Lumumba Friendship University**, where students from every corner of the world study.

Lenin Prospekt is a ceremonial highway to the city. It is along this avenue that heads of state and government and other guests of honour make their entry into the city. Sometimes it is referred to as Space Avenue, as it was along Lenin Prospekt that the first Soviet cosmonauts entered Moscow.

You can reach it by walking along Vorobyovskoye Highway from Leninskiye Gory Metro station to Gagarin Square, or you can take the Metro to Leninsky Prospekt station.

Now let us return to the Lenin Hills and have a look at the new buildings of Moscow Lomonosov University, which has had a galaxy of famous teachers and alumni who have founded new scientific schools and fields—Stoletov, Sechenov, Chaplygin, Timiryazev, Zelinsky, Lebedev, Vernadsky, Zhukovsky, Fortunatov, Kolmogorov, Lavrentyev, Vavilov, Tamm, Kapitsa, Nesmeyanov, Khokhlov, and others.

Since the Revolution Moscow University has trained over 130,000 graduates in various fields, that is, 50 per cent more than in its whole 150 years before the Revolution. Today its 16 departments have over 30,000 undergraduates and post-graduate students of 50 Soviet nationalities, and 2,500 students from 102 other countries. The University is also a research institution. The staff includes over 100 full and corresponding members of the USSR Academy of Sciences, 700 professors, and 2,500 Candidates of Science, famous for their work in the most important fields of modern science.

The new building of Moscow University was put up in 1949-53. Before construction began, this whole area lay on the outskirts of the city. Today the University campus covers an area of 320 hectares, and includes some forty blocks and research facilities. There are also botanical gardens, a sports stadium, and a big park. The chief architects of the main building, the centre of the architectural ensemble, were Lev Rudnev, Sergei Chernyshov, and Pavel Abrosimov. The 32-storey main tower, with its spire crowned by a golden star set in ears of wheat, is 380 metres high. On the flanking 18- and 12-storey blocks there are clocks with surface diameters around nine metres. At a height of more than 100 metres there are statues of a worker and a collective-farm woman, and above them the USSR state emblem. The building contains an assembly hall seating 1,500, a hostel with 6,000 rooms for students, a student club, 19 lecture theatres and 140 auditoriums, dozens of laboratories, a museum of soil science, a large library, a swimming pool, and several gyms.

A Walk of Fame leading up to the main building is flanked on both sides by busts of great Russian scientists. In front of the building are the statues of a young man and a woman by Vera Mukhina (in front of the main entrance) and a monument to the founder, Mikhail Lomonosov, by Nikolai Tomsky, which stands in the inner courtyard.

And now let us look at Moscow from the observation platform. Moscow encircles you, and you are now relatively close to the centre of the city, so much has it grown in the past few decades. Half a century ago its boundary ran more or less along the red and white walls of the Novodevichy Convent and the Circular Railway, which you can clearly see from here.

In various parts of the panorama you can see the silhouettes of tall buildings, and straight ahead in the distance the golden domes of the Kremlin cathedrals and the Ivan the Great Bell Tower. To the right is the Metro bridge. To the left on the horizon are the new blocks of Kalinin Prospekt, the building of the Council for Mutual Economic Assistance, and the Ukraine Hotel. On a clear day, you can see the TV Tower at Ostankino. And down below the Moskva River flows quietly along between its granite embankments.

Between the river and the Circular Railway can be seen the white buildings of the *Lenin Central Stadium at Luzhniki, stretching over a wide area amid green parkland. It took only 15 months to build on a site which was formerly wasteland and meadow (hence the name *Luzhniki*, for *Lug* in Russian means meadow), and which was frequently flooded when the river overflowed its banks. Because of the danger of flooding the area set aside for the building of the stadium—187 hectares in all—had first to be raised 1.5 metres. In the centre of the complex is the Big Bowl. To the right of this you can see a swimming pool and to the left the Small Bowl. Behind it stands the Palace of Sports. Further details about the sports complex at Luzhniki and other Olympic complexes can be read in the chapter "The Moscow Olympics" (see pp. 137-146).

All Muscovites are very fond of the Lenin Hills, where they come to relax with their families. It is pleasant to sit here in summer in the shade of trees, or to walk down the river bank along the forest paths. In winter the Lenin Hills are a favourite spot for skiing and tobogganing.

Our visit to the Lenin Hills is about finished. We are only left to remind you that the easier way back to the centre of Moscow is by Metro from Leninskiye Gory station.

49

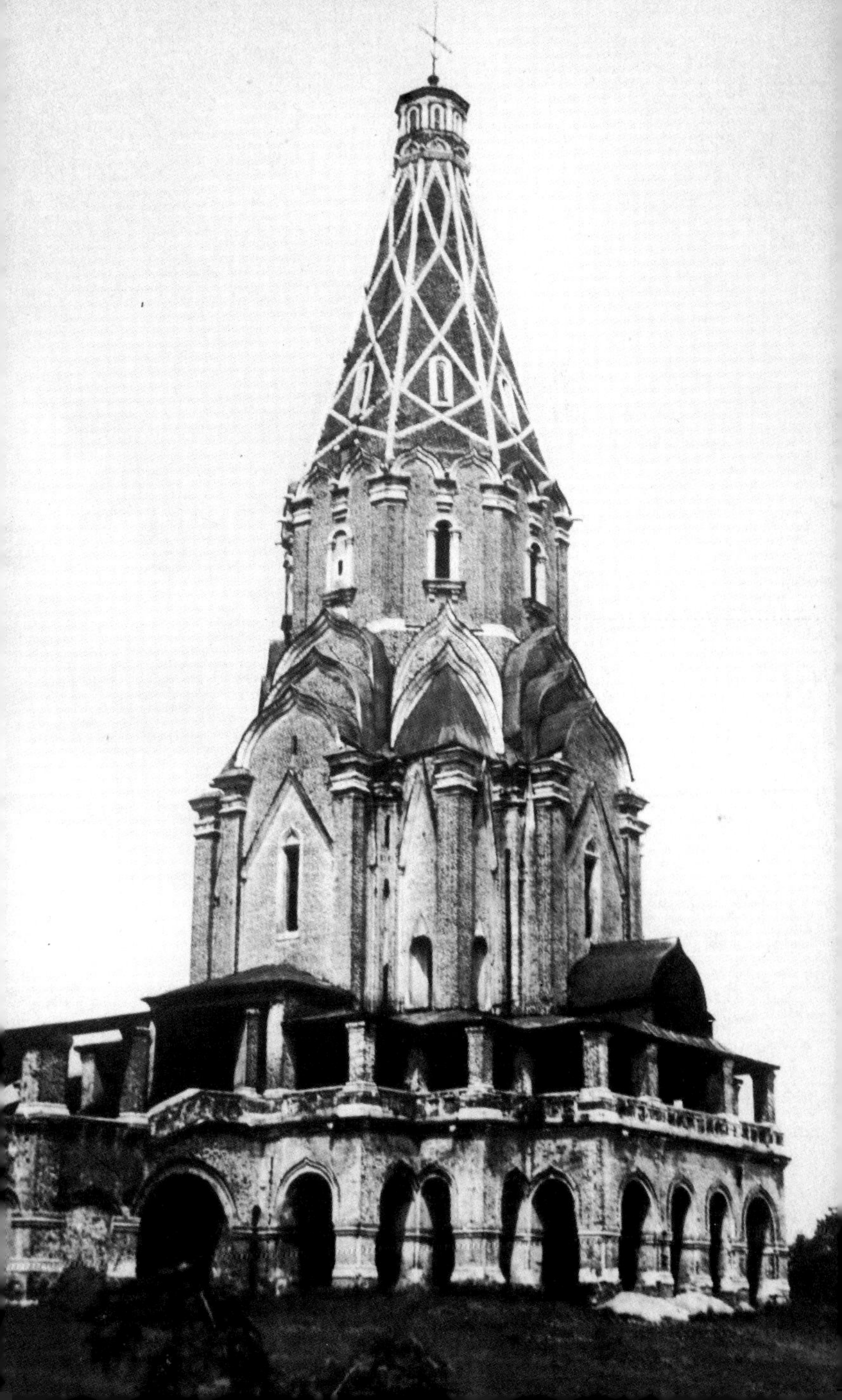

THE MOSCOW OLYMPICS

Muscovites are great sports fans, with one-fifth of the capital's population going in for sport on a regular basis.

P.T. lessons start in the first form. Childrens' and youth sports schools of which there are over one hundred and thirty, are highly popular. Some are all-round sports schools and some specialise in some specific sport. For the latter pupils are selected by experienced coaches and teachers. Children are not allowed to attend if they have poor marks in school. Thus, sport not only helps children to grow agile and strong but assists their spiritual development, too.

Every higher educational establishment in Moscow has its own sports department. The students' sports groups are probably the largest in the capital.

All the city's industrial enterprises and state institutions have sports sections which form part of the trade unions' sports societies. Factory and office workers at over six thousand of the capital's enterprises and institutions daily do P.T. exercises at their place of work. Moscow was the first to start up sports groups for elderly people on an all-Union scale.

There are many different sports facilities in the Soviet capital. The city has 60 large stadiums, 1,335 gyms, 25 swimming pools, 350 football pitches, 2,000 volleyball and basketball courts, two velodromes and a rowing canal.

Major competitions, USSR, European and World championships of various sports and friendly international meetings are held in Moscow. In 1973 the capital played host to the competitors of the Universiada–the World Students' Games.

Soviet athletes first took part in the Olympic Games in Helsinki in 1952; they brought in the spirit and principles of the policy of peaceful co-existence, true friendship and peace among nations to the Olympic movement. Soviet sportsmen have subsequently taken part at the Olympics in Melbourne, Rome, Tokyo, Mexico, Munich and Montreal. Muscovites have performed successfully among the Soviet Olympic competitors and altogether have won 141 gold, 150 silver and 135 bronze medals.

Muscovites, like all Soviet people, welcomed the decision of the International Olympic Committee to hold the summer games of the 22nd Olympics in Moscow, as a tribute to the service of Soviet sport in the Olympic movement. Its inhabitants have actively helped to get the capital ready for the Olympic Games. A vast amount of work has been done in the city to create all the facilities for the sports competitions and for the recreation of guests and tourists and participants. Many new sports facilities and hotels have appeared in Moscow.

Nothing, however, has been built just for the Olympic Games. From the very outset it was decided that all the facilities built for the 1980 Olympic Games would subsequently for many decades be used by the Muscovites for physical training, sport and public activities. The construction of virtually all the sports facilities and many other buildings was stipulated by the city's general development plan and the coming Olympics in Moscow has only accelerated the fulfilment of plans charted previously.

Without disturbing Moscow's development plans, it was decided to build six Olympic sports complexes in the capital. The main sports complex is based at the Lenin Stadium in Luzhniki whose large arena will serve as the main Olympic stadium. The second complex is situated in the vicinity of Leningrad Prospekt where the existing large sports buildings have been supplemented by two new ones. The third complex in Krylatskoye contains a rowing canal, indoor velodrome, a road for cycle racing and an archery field. The fourth complex in the vicinity of Mira Prospekt consists of an indoor stadium and indoor swimming pools. The fifth complex is in Izmailovo, Sokolniki and Mytishchi. The sixth equestrian complex is in the Bitsa forest-park.

Vnukovo and Domodedovo airports have been considerably reconstructed and a new terminal has been built at Sheremetyevo in time for the opening of the Moscow Olympic Games. We should also mention large new buildings such as the Olympic television and radio complex at Ostankino, the Main Press Centre in Zubovsky Boulevard, the International Post Office on the Warsaw Highway and, last but not least, the Olympic Village in the capital's southwestern district—the greatest achievement of the Olympic construction work. Soviet people have done a great deal to ensure that the Moscow Olympic Games is a world-wide celebration of youth, sport, human beauty and friendship among peoples.

Some of the Olympic buildings may rightly be called sights of the capital.

THE MAIN STADIUMS
OF THE 1980 OLYMPICS

The Central Lenin Stadium, the largest stadium not only of the Soviet Union but of Europe, has played host to sportsmen from all over the world. It covers an area of about 180 hectares and consists of The Large and Small Sports Arenas, a swimming pool, a Palace of Sport, a gym with courts for tennis and other games.

The Large Sports Arena contains a football pitch (104 m × 69 m), a 400-metre running track and four track and field sections. This is where the opening and closing ceremonies of the 1980 Olympics, and the finals of the football and track and field athletics competitions will be held and equestrians will compete for the Nations' Prize.

The stands, which guarantee excellent visibility from all angles, hold 103,000 spectators. Part of the stadium is covered, thus protecting spectators and journalists in bad weather. A bowl containing an Olympic flame, which will flare up the moment the Olympics are declared open, will be placed in the arena.

The Small Sports Arena has been considerably reconstructed. A new indoor sports arena has been built within the framework of the existing outdoor one. This is where volleyball competitions will be held during the Games. The stands now hold 10,000 people.

The building of the indoor swimming pool architecturally harmonises with the Small Sports Arena. The water-polo competitions will take place here.

The Palace of Sport with a rectangular arena (61 m by 30 m) is situated a short distance away from the main buildings of the Central Stadium. This is where the gymnastics and judo competitions will be held during the Games.

The most prominent new building of the sports complex is the originally designed Universal Hall. From the outside it looks like a huge tortoise shell on twenty-eight reinforced-concrete legs. Inside there is an arena whose size and shape may be changed to suit any of the twelve types of sports competitions to be held here. The stands may also be rearranged to seat from 1,500 to 3,900 spectators. The voleyball tournament will be held here during the 1980 Olympics. The Universal Hall is a highly spectacular sight both in the day-time and at night, especially if viewed from the Metro Bridge and Lenin Hills.

THE SPORTS COMPLEX IN THE VICINITY OF LENINGRAD PROSPEKT

Leningrad Prospekt is one of the capital's widest and most attractive boulevards. Several large sports complexes are situated along it, the oldest of which, the Dynamo Stadium, was built in 1923. During the Olympics this complex will be used for training sessions of many types of sport, and the preliminary football games will be played on its main pitch.

Nearby the Dynamo Stadium is the Young Pioneers' Stadium. By the 1980 Olympics it will have been considerably renovated. Among its facilities is a velodrome with stands for 10,000 spectators which will be used for training. It also has a pitch (102 m by 65 m) for the Olympic grass hockey matches with stands for 5,000 fans of this relatively new sport in Moscow. Dinamo Metro Station is the nearest to the Dynamo and Young Pioneers' stadiums.

Not far from the Young Pioneers' Stadium is the Central Army Sports Club (nearest Metro Station—Aeroport). The complex consists of a Sports Palace, where Soviet ice-hockey players and figure skaters train, a swimming pool with eight fifty-metre lanes, and a heavy athletics section with gyms for gymnastics, boxing, fencing and tennis competitions, to name but a few. By the 1980 Olympics this complex will be supplemented by a football pitch and track and field facilities for the Graeco-Roman wrestling and fencing competitions. In one of the building's wings there is a track and field section (126 m by 84 m) with four two-hundred-metre circular tracks with a synthetic turf. Here, too, are javelin- and discus-throwing, long and high jump sections. In another wing of the building there is a football pitch (102 m by 60 m) also with a synthetic covering. During the Olympics seventeen fencing strips and one special strip for the finals will be marked out on the pitch. Subsequently, archery competitions may also be held here. The stands and balcony hold 5,880 spectators.

A new all-purpose gym, where the hand-ball competitions will be held, has been built in Lavochkin Street (nearest Metro station—Rechnoi Vokzal), a few minutes' ride away from the Central Army Sports Club along Leningrad Prospekt. After the Olympics it will be used for national and international competitions in twelve types of sport.

THE OLYMPIC COMPLEX
AT KRYLATSKOYE

A rowing canal was built a few years ago in a bend on the Moskva River to the southwest of the city centre. Within a short space of time this canal has become world-famous. An artificial riverbed was dug for the canal which enabled it to be positioned according to prevailing winds in the best possible way and its stands for 3,400 spectators to be arranged in the most practical manner. By the Olympic Games new stands will have been built and 20,000 spectators will be able to watch all the various rowing competitions. The canal is unique in size: it is 2,300 metres long and up to 125 metres wide. A seventy-five-metre wide canal marked with buoys along which the boats may return runs parallel to the main canal.

The first Soviet indoor cycle track with stands for 6,000 spectators is situated near the canal. The track is 333.33 metres long and its surface is inlaid with special high-quality sorts of wood. All kinds of competitions, ranging from sprints to marathon pursuit races may be held on the track.

For the first time in the history of the Olympic Games a circuit road for cycle racing has been built very near the velodrome. The track is 13.5 kilometres long, 7 metres wide and the straight finishing stretch is 14 metres long.

The Olympic complex also has a special archery field with 92 targets and stands for 3,000 spectators. Krylatskoye is now a favourite recreation spot and sports centre for thousands of Muscovites. Special buses run between the complex and Molodyozhnaya Metro station.

THE OLYMPIC COMPLEX IN THE VICINITY
OF MIR PROSPEKT

This is the largest sports complex to be built in Moscow for the Olympic Games. Its construction was, however, planned long before Moscow was chosen for the setting of the 1980 Olympics. It consists of an indoor stadium with stands for 45,000 spectators and indoor swimming pools with stands for 10,000 spectators.

THE MOSCOW OLYMPICS

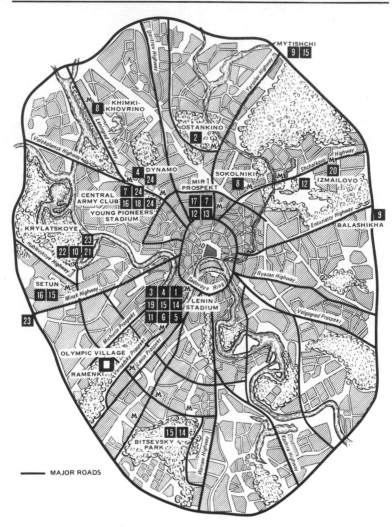

1 — Olimpiada ACS
2 — Radio and TV Centre
3 — Athletics
4 — Football
5 — Gymnastics
6 — Volleyball
7 — Basketball
8 — Handball
9 — Shooting
10 — Archery
11 — Water Polo
12 — Diving

13 — Swimming
14 — Equestrian Sports
15 — Modern Pentathlon
16 — Fencing
17 — Boxing
18 — Wrestling
19 — Judo
20 — Weightlifting
21 — Rowing
22 — Cycling
23 — Canoeing
24 — Hockey

The complex, which covers 20 hectares, is situated between Shchep-kin Street and Durov Street and two new main roads. The main entrance for spectators using public transport is near Prospekt Mira Metro station. The complex may be reached from the city centre by a new main road running along Neglinnaya Street, Tsvetnoi and Samotechny boulevards.

The oval-shaped indoor stadium and building containing the swimming pools were built on the same axis with the same base. Boxing and volleyball competitions will be held in the indoor stadium during the Games. The sports arena has been specially designed to divide into two separate halves (with the help of an acoustic partition) so that these competitions may be held simultaneously. The sports arena of the indoor stadium is 127 by 91 metres in size. It contains a football pitch with an artificial surface which after the Olympics may be iced over for ice-hockey games and figure skating. The left part of the stadium, which is intended for the Olympic boxing matches, has stands for 18,000 spectators; the stands on the right-hand side of the stadium, which are to be used by the Olympic basketball players, holds 16,000 spectators.

The building housing the swimming pools complements the indoor stadium and its architecture is therefore plainer and simpler. Some of the Olympic swimming and diving competitions will be held here. The building consists of three sports sections. The first section with a pool of 33 by 25 metres and 6 to 4 metres deep is for the diving competitions and its stands hold 5,000 people. The second section with a pool of 50 by 25 metres and 2 metres deep is for the swimming competitions which may be watched by 9,000 spectators. The third is for training sessions. The building also has three smaller pools, two training pools for leading competitors, and recreation rooms.

THE SPORTS COMPLEXES IN IZMAILOVO, SOKOLNIKI AND MYTISHCHI

A new all-purpose gym and swimming pool have been constructed by the junction of Shchelkovskoye Highway and Sirenevy Boulevard (nearest Metro Station—Izmailovsky Park), close by one of the world's largest forest-parks covering an area of 1,200 hectares. The country's largest sports training centre—the Lenin Institute of Physical Education—is also situated in Izmailovo.

During the Olympics heavy athletics competitions, which may be watched by 5,000 spectators, will take place in the all-purpose gym. The gym also has training and recreation rooms for the sportsmen, a press centre and a first-aid post. The building, especially its three-millimetre-thick large span roof of stainless steel, is originally designed.

The Sokolniki sports complex is located near the Izmailovo complex. Its main facility is the Sokolniki Palace of Sport in whose arena twenty different sports may be contested. The Palace will be used for the Olympic hand-ball competitions.

The Dynamo shooting-range is situated to the northwest of Sokolniki, five kilometres from the Ring Road in the town of Mytishchi. During the Games the pistol and skeet shooting competitions will be held here. The complex consists of a fifty-metre shooting-range with ninety targets and a twenty-five-metre range with sixteen targets, three moving targets and four shooting-ranges for skeet shooting with stands.

THE EQUESTRIAN COMPLEX IN THE BITSA FOREST-PARK

An equestrian complex has been opened in a picturesque park between Warsaw Highway and Profsoyuznaya Street on the south side of the city. It may be reached by Balaklavsky Prospekt and the nearest Metro stations are Kakhovskaya and Kaluzhskaya.

All the equestrian sports included in the Olympic programme, except the individual show jumping event, will be held here. The complex has stands for 12,000 spectators, a 1,800-metre steeplechase circuit with stands for 1,500, a dressage field with stands for 1,000 and an indoor exercise ring (90 m by 38 m) with stands for 2,000 people.

A gym, swimming pool and shooting-range have been built at Bitsa for the pentathlon sportsmen.

All the facilities of the equestrian complex not only meet the sports requirements in every way but also harmonise well with the large forest-park's natural surroundings.

THE OLYMPIC VILLAGE

The Olympic Village, an attractive architectural ensemble consisting of eighteen sixteen-storey apartment blocks, is located at the end of Michurin Prospekt in the southwest district of the capital. The 12,800 members of the national sports delegations will be accommodated here. The blocks consist of two- and three-room apartments equipped with every up-to-date convenience. Soviet architects made a study of previous Olympics when planning the Olympic Village. Special care has been taken to provide the sportsmen not only with excellent conditions for relaxation but also for training. The Village adjoins a sports complex consisting of various all-purpose gyms, several swimming pools, volleyball, basketball and tennis courts, a football pitch and a track and field section.

The restaurants, cafés and canteens may cater for 4,000 people at any one time. The Village has its own shopping centre, international post office, bank, automatic telephone exchange with 20,000 numbers, clinic, chemist's, information bureau for every sport, special rooms with telemonitors and colour televisions, and a commuterised board with regular relays of the latest news from all the Olympic competitions.

The Village's cultural centre consists of a concert hall seating 1,200, two cinemas, a dance hall, discotecque, amusement hall and library.

After the Olympics all these amenities will be turned over to Muscovites and the Village will become one of the new residential districts of the city.

The Village is ideally situated. It takes only fifteen minutes by car from here to the Lenin Stadium at Luzhniki or the rowing canal and cycle circuit track at Krylatskoye. The nearest Metro station is Yugo-Zapadnaya.

THE MAIN PRESS CENTRE AND TELEVISION AND RADIO COMPLEX

The Main Press Centre of the 1980 Olympics is located in Zubovsky Boulevard near Park Kultury Metro station. The building is next to the Proviantskiye Store Houses, a monument of Russian architecture, which was built in the first half of the 19th century after the design of the architect

Stasov. Opposite the Press Centre is Progress Publishers, who incidentally put out this guide book.

The Main Press Centre's six-storey building is harmoniously inscribed in the architecture along the Sadovoye Ring.

Up to 3,000 journalists and 500 photographers will be able to work in the building which has every convenience. The foreign and Soviet journalists accredited here will be allotted rooms and essential equipment. From here they will be able to contact their editing offices directly by telephone, relay material by telegraph, phototelegraph and telex. Special bus services will connect the Main Press Centre with all the Olympic complexes.

After the Olympics Novosti Press Agency and the Soviet Journalists' Union will be located here.

A new television and radio complex has been built five hundred metres away from the unique Ostankino Television Tower. It consists of a five-storey building of studios connected to a fourteen-storey switchboard centre. The new television and radio complex has been supplied with the most up-to-date scientific and technical equipment. Live television coverage of the competitions will be relayed on 18 to 20 channels to every part of the world. What's more, the Olympic television and radio complex will broadcast one hundred radio programmes.

After the Olympics the reconstructed television centre will relay television programmes to remote parts of the country at convenient times for viewers.

The new sports complexes, large hotels and other public facilities will significantly enhance the architecture of the Soviet capital. Since some of its streets have been reconstructed, numerous historical and cultural architectural monuments restored, parks enlarged, and new gardens have been laid, Moscow has become even more beautiful and imposing.

IF YOU HAVE AN EXTRA DAY...

Moscow has many places of interest. We believe we have already described the most interesting ones that should be visited first. In choosing them we did not forget that you may not have very much time for sightseeing; but if you should have an extra day to spare, here are some suggestions.

A Tour of the Metro

The *Moscow Metro is not only a convenient means of transport but also a unique engineering and architectural structure. We have already mentioned a number of its stations in describing walks around the city. We shall now tell you more about the Metropolitan Railway as one of the city's major sights in itself.

> Plans to build an underground railway in Moscow were talked about before the Revolution. The City Duma looked into a project in 1902, but rejected it. "This project," the newspaper *Russkoye Slovo* wrote, "is a staggeringly impudent encroachment on everything Russian people hold dear in the city of Moscow. As the tunnel of the metropolitan railway will pass in places only a few feet beneath churches, the peace and quiet of these sacred places will be disturbed."

A Metro was begun in Moscow only in Soviet times. The first shaft was sunk in 1931 and the first train ran on May 15, 1935, when the first thirteen stations were opened. Steady building and extension continued, and did not stop even in the hard days of the war. Today the Moscow Metro (which bears the name of Lenin) has over a hundred stations.

The layout of the Metro reflects the traditional structure of the city, several lines radiating from the centre, and linked by a circle line (see the diagram on the fly-leaf). According to the general plan for the development of the city, the number of stations will increase greatly, and the length of the system will then be around 320 kilometres.

The Metro is the quickest way of getting across Moscow. It connects the centre with all districts, including areas of intensive new housing development. Its trains carry over five million passengers daily. Their speed reaches 90 kilometres an hour on some sectors; at rush hour the interval between them is only 50 or 70 seconds.

Several thousand trains a day are operated. Up-to-date rolling stock and other equipment and a well-organised service ensure punctuality and safety. An automatic train control system employing computers helps the drivers, who only have to see that the controls are set and operating properly.

Most of the stations are deep underground, but there are sections of the line that are on the surface. There is a ventilation system in the tunnels and stations.

No two stations are alike; each has its own architectural and artistic design. They are light, spacious, and of a cleanliness that gladdens the eye. Valuable types of stone and wood from various parts of the Russian Federation and other republics have been used to face the halls, tunnels, and escalators of the stations. You could say that the whole country built, and is building, the Moscow Metro.

Take *Kropotkinskaya*, a station designed by Alexei Dushkin and Yakov Lichtenberg. Its architecture is simple and expressive, and gives you the impression that it is not underground at all but filled with sunshine. *Mayakovskaya*, also by Dushkin, is quite different. Its red marble columns edged with light steel strips give it an air of grandeur and elegance. The vaulting has mosaics executed to cartoons by Alexander Deineka. Also of interest is *Komsomolskaya* on the Circle Line, designed by two men renowned in Soviet art, the architect Alexei Shchusev and the artist Pavel Korin. The station is 190 metres long and nine metres high; its vaults are supported on 72 pillars. The colourful decoration and eight large mosaics of the hall reflect the Soviet people's struggle for independence.

The more recent additions to the Metro are rather different in style, simpler in their architecture and more modest in decor.

Here is a route that will enable you to visit stations most characteristic of the time of their construction: *Ploshchad Revolutsii*–transfer to *Ploshchad Sverdlova*–*Mayakovskaya*–*Belorusskaya*–transfer to the Circle *(Koltsevaya)* Line–*Kievskaya*–transfer to the Arbatsko-Pokrovskaya Line–*Arbatskaya*–*Kurskaya*–transfer to the Circle Line–*Komsomolskaya*–transfer to the Radial Line–*Prospekt Marxa*. The whole journey will take about 90 minutes.

Book your Metro excursion through the service bureau in your hotel. A simple way of sampling the Metro independently is to travel five or six stops from the station nearest your hotel, getting out of the train at each station to look round the platform. But don't try this at rush hour. The best times for exploring the

Metro are in the morning between 10:00 and 12:00, in the afternoon between 14:00 and 17:00, and in the evening after 20:00. The Metro operates from 6:00 to 1:00. Transfer from one station to another ends at 1:00 sharp. The fare, regardless of the distance travelled, is five kopecks.

A Boat Trip on the River

The Moskva River is 502 kilometres long and flows through the city for 80 kilometres. Various launches, motor ships, and hydrofoils provide trips of varying length throughout the summer till late autumn. We suggest you begin a trip at the **pier on Berezhkovskaya Embankment**, which is near Kiev Railway Station, five to seven minutes' walk from Kievskaya Metro station. If you take a river boat downstream from here, you would be advised to get off at the **pier on Moskvoretskaya Embankment**, near the Rossia Hotel (nearest Metro station Ploshchad Nogina). The trip, which costs 30 kopecks, will take about an hour and a half.

From the bow of the boat you will see historical and cultural monuments, new residential areas, picturesque parks and gardens, beaches, embankments, and bridges—many of which you have not yet managed to see. You will pass close to the churches and towers of the Novodevichy Convent, the Lenin Central Stadium at Luzhniki, the Gorky Central Park, the Kremlin cathedrals and palaces, and the Rossia Hotel.

The water of the Moskva River is clean enough for fish. You will see anglers casting their lines direct from the parapet of the embankments, and fishing not just for small fry.

A river trip is a real treat and the best time is in the afternoon when it is not so hot.

Museum Estates

Kolomenskoye—this was the manor of Kolomenskoye and is a monument of 16th- and 17th-century culture. It was the Moscow estate of Russian princes and tsars, including Ivan the Terrible and Peter the Great. The Church of the Ascension (1532) is a fine example of old Russian architecture.

The museum is open daily, except Tuesdays, from 11:00 to 17:00, admission 20 kopecks. You can get there by Metro to Kolomenskaya Station.

Kuskovo and the Ceramics Museum—this is a fine specimen of 18th-century art and architecture, and has a collection of ceramics, porcelain, pottery, majolica, and glass of various periods.

The museum is open on Wednesdays, Thursdays, and Fridays from 11:00 to 19:00, and on Saturdays and Sundays from 10:00 to 18:00, but is closed on the last Wednesday of the month. Admission 30 kopecks. To get there, take the Metro to Zhdanovskaya Station.

A Visit to the Countryside Around Moscow

Moscow is surrounded by picturesque forests, fields, oak woods, meandering rivers, azure lakes, and man-made reservoirs. A visit is not only worth it for its own beauty, there are also memorable places just outside Moscow associated with Russian history and the country's revolutionary past and culture.

It is not easy to describe all the areas around Moscow in limited compass, so we shall confine ourselves to a few spots that are especially worth visiting.

GORKI LENINSKIYE

About 35 kilometres south of Moscow on Kashira Highway is the **Gorki Estate**, a mansion on a high hill in an extensive park of old trees. From

September 1918 Lenin frequently went there to rest and relax, and lived there from May 1923 until his death on January 21, 1924.

On the 25th anniversary of Lenin's death a memorial museum was opened on the Gorki Estate. The Soviet people have kept the memory of Lenin sacred. Everything at Gorki has been kept as it was during his life-time: the two-storey wing, where he lived upstairs with his family; the central building where he lived the last months of his life; and his favourite spots, in particular the round summerhouse not far from the house.

Lenin's room is very simply furnished, and has nothing superfluous: an upholstered arm-chair, a small table with inkstand, paper knife, spectacles, and several books. One of the books is a volume of stories by Jack London (Love of Life) that his wife, Nadezhda Krupskaya, was reading to him two days before he died. In the left-hand corner is a wooden bed covered with a quilt. Between the window and the bed is a mirror with a glass shelf on which stand a lamp, a small nickel-plated bell, a glass, and some medicine bottles. Everything somehow reflects Lenin's modesty, and we can see the truth of Gorky's statement about him that he was the most humane and simple man.

Delegates from the workers and peasants of Soviet Russia, anxiously following the state of Lenin's health during his illness, used to come to see him at Gorki. In November 1923, he was visited by a delegation of textile workers, who brought him a gift of a red calico shirt made by their finest weavers, and 18 cherry saplings. In their accompanying letter they wrote: "May these cherry trees freshly planted in your garden bring you speedy recovery."

Among Lenin's visitors were Maxim Gorky, Romain Rolland, Martin Andersen Nexö, and Henri Barbusse.

On New Year's Eve, 1923-24, Lenin asked for a New Year's tree to be set up in Gorki for the children of the local peasants; and he saw the New Year in with them, cheerfully watching them singing and dancing.

Three weeks later, at 6:50 p.m. on January 21, he passed away. A man thus died who, as Henri Barbusse wrote, "was the embodiment of the whole Russian revolution, who conceived it in his mind, prepared it, carried it through, and saved it—Lenin, the greatest, and in every way the most honest of the creators of history, a man who did more for the people than anyone else".

ARKHANGELSKOYE ESTATE

The *Arkhangelskoye Estate is a highly interesting architectural monument of the 18th-19th century in picturesque surroundings on the bank of the Moskva River. It is located 16 kilometres out from Moscow on Volokolamsk Highway and then along the road to Petrovo-Dalneye.

The whole ensemble of Arkhangelskoye—palace, park, theatre, and service buildings—took forty years to build and lay out. The first gardens were laid out at the end of the 17th century. In 1810, the land passed into the hands of Prince Yusupov, the director of the imperial theatres and the Hermitage. When purchasing works for the Hermitage, Yusupov kept himself in mind, and turned his palace near Moscow into a real museum displaying wonderful work by talented painters, sculptors, and folk artists.

The centrepiece of the estate is the palace built in classical style by well-known Russian architects, but the real creators of the whole ensemble were the gifted craftsmen among Yusupov's serfs, above all, the serf architect Vassily Strizhakov.

The palace stands at the highest point on the estate and overlooks the park, which slopes down to the Moskva River in terraces.

The main courtyard of Arkhangelskoye is framed by the wing colonnades of the central building. The halls of the palace are sumptuously decorated and furnished with antique sculptures, tapestries, and porcelain, incrusted furniture, cut-glass chandeliers, numerous mirrors, murals, and a multi-patterned parquet.

The palace is surrounded by a splendid park, its walks embellished with sculptures, decorative stairways, colonnades, pavilions, and arbours. A triumphal arch, built in 1817, stands at the entrance to the estate.

After the October Revolution, Arkhangelskoye was nationalised and taken under state protection as a valuable monument of Russian culture. Restoration work, begun in 1933, returned palace and park to their original appearance. In 1937 two buildings were erected in the grounds as a rest home.

Today Arkhangelskoye is a splendid museum with a valuable art collection. It is probably the most complete manor around Moscow. In the building of the serf theatre, built in 1819, there is a permanent exhibition on the serf theatre of Arkhangelskoye.

Near the main entrance there is a restaurant where you can order Russian dishes made from bear's meat and game.

A visit to Arkhangelskoye is a fine outing. The road to it passes through forests of conifers, nut groves, and glades, and in places runs very close to the Moskva River.

BORODINO

On August 26, 1812, a tremendous battle took place on a field near the village of Borodino between Napoleon's troops and the Russian army commanded by Mikhail Kutuzov.

Napoleon hurled 135,000 soldiers and 587 guns against the Russian army, which had 120,000 men and 640 guns before the battle.

The battle lasted 15 hours. It was a heroic page in the history of the Russian people's struggle for freedom and independence. The Russian officers and men, who vowed to fight to the end, displayed great courage, fortitude and patriotism.

Here, for the first time, Napoleon failed to win a decisive battle, and he himself realised this: "The Russians won the right to be called invincible."

The Battle of Borodino changed the tide of the war in favour of the Russian army. After Borodino, the French army was unable to recover, even after occupying Moscow, which had been abandoned by the Russians.

The village of Borodino is 124 kilometres from Moscow on Minsk Highway. Monuments to the courage and heroism of the Russian soldiers have been erected on the historic battlefield, most of them in 1912, to mark the centenary of the battle, from funds contributed by officers and men of Russian army units that had fought there.

A monument to Field Marshal Kutuzov was erected on the spot from where he directed the operations of the Russian army. It is a granite obelisk crowned with a bronze eagle with outspread wings and a laurel wreath. Above the bas-relief portrait of Kutuzov are the words from his dispatch on the results of the battle: "The enemy was repulsed at all points."

Some 150 metres from the Shevardinsky redoubt, where on August 24, two days before the Battle of Borodino, there was fierce fighting between an advanced post of the Russian army and the advancing French regiments, there is a grey granite obelisk with a bronze eagle and an inscription: "To the fallen of the *Grande Armée*." This obelisk was also erected in 1912 with funds raised in France. At the entrance to the memorial chapel to the soldiers of the 1st and 19th Chasseur Regiments of the Russian Army who were killed in action, there is an inscription in gold: "We pledged to die and we kept our oath of loyalty at the Battle of Borodino" (lines taken from a poem by Mikhail Lermontov).

On the Borodino battlefield is the *Borodino Military History Museum with a collection of documents and exhibits relating to this battle and the war of 1812.

Lev Tolstoy visited the battlefield in September 1876, when working on his *War and Peace*. While there, he drew up a plan of the battle between the two armies that he described so authentically in his novel.

Near the monument to Kutuzov is the common grave of Soviet Guardsmen who fell in action against nazi troops in the winter of 1941. The Borodino battlefield was covered with trenches, anti-tank ditches, and other defence works. Only two houses in the large village of Borodino were left standing after the fighting. At present dozens of tourists visit now rebuilt village every single day to honour the heroes' memory.

ZAGORSK

Seventy kilometres north of Moscow on Yaroslavl Highway is the *Zagorsk History and Art Museum, which contains magnificent relics of Russian culture of the 14th to 19th centuries.

The Trinity-St. Sergiy Monastery, built in the 1340s, is one of the oldest around Moscow, and played a major role in the history of Moscow and the Russian state. It was a stronghold that more than once defended the principal city of old Russia from foreign invaders. Its stone fortifications, erected in 1540-80, are 12 metres high. In 1608-10 the defenders of the Monastery, around 3,000 strong, heroically withstood a 16-month siege by 15,000 well-armed Polish soldiers.

In the 16th and 17th centuries the Monastery was a major cultural centre where master icon painters, book copyists, wood carvers, silversmiths, and other craftsmen worked. Wonderful art treasures were kept in its churches. In 1920 a museum was opened in the grounds. Today the Moscow Theological Academy and Seminary are housed in the Monastery.

(The Church in the USSR is divorced from the State. The country has working churches, mosques, synagogues, and various other places of worship. There is a special Council for Religious Affairs under the USSR Council of Ministers.)

The whole ensemble of the Trinity-St. Sergiy Monastery is of exceptional value. Here some of the finest and most characteristic examples of early Russian architecture and painting have been preserved. The most important among them is the white-stone Troitsky (Trinity) Cathedral built in 1422-23 in the early Moscow style. Its façade is adorned with pilasters and a carved stone band. The building is crowned by a huge dome. The paintings of the iconostasis and murals, fragments of which have been preserved to this day, are the work of Andrei Rublev, the great painter of the late 14th and early 15th centuries, and other artists of his school. The

Church of Holy Spirit *(Dukhovskaya Tserkov)*, built in 1476-77, is an unusual building and has a two-tier tower. Bells hang on the lower tier, while the upper serves as an observation platform.

In 1559-85, the monumental five-domed **Cathedral of the Assumption** was built in the Monastery grounds by order of Ivan the Terrible, and came to be considered the principal cathedral of the Monastery. Its architectural forms are similar to those of the Cathedral of the Assumption in the Moscow Kremlin. Seventeenth-century frescoes and an 18th-century iconostasis finely carved, gilded, and painted by Russian artists have been preserved inside.

There are other interesting architectural monuments in the Monastery, among them various service buildings: the Hospital Wards with the hipped-roof Church of Zosima and Savvaty (1635-37), the Tsar's Chambers, the Refectory (17th century), the private chambers of the metropolitan, the bell tower, built in 1741-70, the well chapel, built at the end of the 17th century, with its small carved white-stone columns intertwined with grape vines, and the attractive Smolensk Church, erected in 1745-48.

The road to Zagorsk passes dense forests, collective-farm fields, and the urban areas that have grown up here in Soviet times.

On the way, 43 kilometres from Moscow, is the **Russkaya Skazka** (Russian Fairy tale) **Restaurant**, which we recommend to you.

KLIN

Klin is an old Russian town 84 kilometres north-west of Moscow on Leningrad Highway. It was founded in 1318 on the high bank of the Sestra, a tributary of the Volga. In the grounds of a former monastery there is a church built in the 16th century, and another built in 1712 in the Moscow baroque style.

But Klin is known first and foremost for another reason: it was the home of Tchaikovsky. Thousands of tourists and music-lovers come here to pay tribute to his memory. The house in which he last lived in Klin has been turned into a museum and everything is kept as it was during his life.

It was in Klin that Tchaikovsky composed many of his romances, his ballet *Sleeping Beauty*, the *Hamlet* overture, and the Fifth Symphony. He also worked on *The Nutcracker* here and composed the Sixth Symphony, a masterpiece of world symphony music.

> Tchaikovsky was very fond of Klin, of its tranquility and landscape. "I can't say how terribly attached I have become to Klin," he wrote, "and I just can't imagine myself anywhere else. I find no words to express how much I feel the charm of the Russian countryside, the Russian landscape, and this quiet that I need more than anything else."

Many visiting composers and musicians come to Klin. Twice a year, on the anniversaries of Tchaikovsky's birth and death, leading Soviet and foreign musicians sit down at his piano there and play his music.

The museum is surrounded by a garden with large, tall trees that form shady walks along which Tchaikovsky used to enjoy strolling.

The house has an interesting history. After the composer's death, one of his friends and assistants bought it from the merchant who owned it, so that it could be kept intact. In 1920 a society of friends of the Tchaikovsky Museum was organised.

During World War II the house underwent a terrible ordeal. Nazi troops who had occupied Klin in 1941 ravaged it. Following liberation of the town the house was restored and on May 7, 1945, Tchaikovsky's birthday, the museum was reopened to the endless visitors who find inexhaustible joy and inspiration in his music.

 In conclusion we would remind you that excursions to the Moscow countryside can be booked through the service bureau in your hotel. The excursions described here take the following time, including the trip there and back: Gorki Leninskiye—four hours; Arkhangelskoye—four and a half hours; Borodino (Saturdays and Sundays only)—eight hours; Zagorsk—six and a half hours; and Klin—seven hours.

INFORMATION

SOME USEFUL HINTS

There is a service bureau in all hotels catering for foreign tourists and visitors. It is open from 9:00 to late in the evening (usually until 22:00). There is always someone on duty who knows several languages.

The service bureau, and the corresponding departments of the Sputnik Youth Travel Agency, the All-Union Central Council of Trade Unions, and other institutions and organisations through which people come to the Soviet Union, can give you the information you need about your stay in the USSR, make reservations for you on excursions and for visits to exhibitions, museums, art galleries, theatres, concert halls, etc. The service bureau has posters with the repertoires of theatres and concert halls for the current ten-day period. Tickets can be ordered in advance through the service bureau. Questions concerning your travel documents and arrangements, trains, routes, and departure times, hotel and restaurant services, etc. can be referred to the service bureau; and they can tell you where shops are located and when they are open.

Every service bureau usually has a desk dealing with transportation matters, where you can get help with plane, train, or ship reservations and tickets, and ordering taxis.

You will find porters at every airport and railway station to carry your luggage. There is a standard charge for their services of 30 kopecks a piece.

There are no night clubs in Moscow. Restaurants close at 23:00 (a few at midnight). Certain hotels (Intourist, Metropole, National, and some others) have bars that are open until 2:00. Some restaurants and cafés have orchestras and dance floors.

Evening performances at theatres and concert halls begin at 19:00 or 19:30, and finish between 22:00 or 23:00. It is customary to check your hat and coat at the theatre. There is no charge for this service. Opera glasses can be hired for a small charge (30 or 40 kopecks).

Cinemas are open from 9:00 until about midnight. Ticket holders are only admitted in the intervals between programmes (or between the shorts and the main feature film). The programme usually consists of a newsreel (or a short film), and a full-length feature film, and lasts about two hours. It is not customary at cinemas to check your hat and coat. Smoking is not permitted in the auditorium. Seats are numbered and reserved.

Dance halls in parks and public gardens close at 23:00.

The monetary unit in the Soviet Union is the ruble. It is made up of 100 kopecks. The coinage consists of one-, two-, three-, five-, ten-, 15-, 20- and 50-kopeck pieces, and one ruble coins. Paper money consists of one-, three-, five-, ten-, 25-, 50- and 100-ruble notes.

Factory and office workers in the Soviet Union have a five-day (41-hour) working week, except in enterprises with continuous production processes. The working day in factories usually begins at 8:00 but at 9:00 a.m. in offices, and is eight hours long. Working days preceding national holidays are one hour shorter. Lunch-breaks, mostly an hour in length, fall between 12:00 and 15:00.

The national holidays (non-working days) of the USSR are January 1 (New Year's Day), March 8 (International Women's Day), May 1 and 2 (day of international solidarity of working people), May 9 (Victory Day over German fascism), October 7 (Constitution Day), and November 7 and 8 (the anniversary of the Great October Socialist Revolution).

Shops dealing in consumer goods, gifts, etc. usually open at 11:00 and close at 20:00. Big department stores open at 8:00 and close at 21:00. Almost all shops of this kind are closed on Sundays. Food shops are open every day from 9:00 to 20:00, with some closing only at 22:00. On Sundays and national holidays they shut two hours earlier.

MEDICAL SERVICES

Medical care is free in the USSR and available to everyone in town and country. Foreigners who fall ill during their stay in the USSR are given free medical treatment, but if they have to be hospitalised, they are charged in line with the practice adopted in most other countries. Except in emergencies, tourists are only admitted to hospital on a doctor's recommendation.

If you feel unwell, please notify your Intourist interpreter or the hotel service bureau so that a doctor can be called. There is no charge for the doctor's visit, but any medicines prescribed must be bought at a pharmacy at the current prices.

If you are arranging to come to the Soviet Union for treatment, we advise you to find out from the appropriate department of Intourist ... or the local tourist organisation, what medical formalities you need to comply with to obtain the necessary documents (doctor's certificate on your general state of health, vaccination certificate, and so on).

FILMING AND PHOTOGRAPHY

In Moscow, and elsewhere in the USSR, foreign tourists are permitted to photograph or film architectural monuments, streets, squares, blocks of flats, public buildings, theatres, museums, etc. and various sights and landscapes. You can also sketch them.

But it should be borne in mind that, like in other countries, in the USSR there are definite rules for filming and photographing. By observing them you will avoid any misunderstanding.

In the Soviet Union it is prohibited to photograph military objects and equipment, sea ports, bridges, tunnels, radio stations, etc. It is also forbidden to film from on board aircraft.

At factories, farms, and state institutions, photographs may only be taken with the permission of the management.

If you wish to photograph someone, we suggest that you ask permission first, for many people do not like being photographed by strangers.

SOUVENIRS

You will find in the shops a large selection of goods which are characteristic of our country, including handicrafts and manufactured goods.

Handicrafts make splendid souvenirs: wood carvings, bone figurines, painted wooden articles, ceramics, stamped leather, chased, enamelled and filigree metalwork, embroidery, and rugs. The best handicrafts of Soviet craftsmen have many times won prizes at Soviet and international exhibitions.

Palekh lacquer miniatures are very popular. The work of Palekh artists (Palekh is the village where this style of miniature painting was developed) is noted for its finesse, rich range of colours, and highly decorative effect. There are caskets, cigarette cases, powder boxes, and brooches, among other things, all painted on papier-mâché base.

Articles made in the villages of Mstera and Fedoskino are of a similar type. Their miniatures usually depict characters from Russian fairy tales, scenes from urban and rural life, and the Russian scenery.

Russian lace makes an elegant decoration and rare souvenir. In various gift shops you will find lace tablecloths, bed-spreads, pillow cases, napkins, collars and cuffs, and shawls.

The bright red and black wooden articles, with a very attractive pattern on a golden background, invariably attract the attention of souvenir shoppers. They are the work of Khokhloma craftsmen, who have passed their art down from generation to generation for ever 300 years. Khokhloma ware includes wooden cups and spoons, all kinds of goblets, trays and furniture, painted in this traditional and unique style. Khokhloma ware is durable and can be washed in hot water.

Bone carvings (from walrus tusks) by Northern craftsmen make unusual and interesting souvenirs. There are filigree brooches, picture frames, paper knives, caskets, and figurines of various size, depicting animals and scenes from the life of the peoples of the North.

Tourists are attracted by the *matryoshka* wooden dolls, painted in bright colours and polished. Sometimes there are as many as twelve dolls, one inside the other. These original *matryoshka* dolls, which are made near Moscow in Khotkovo and Semyonovo, make a delightful present, and are probably the most popular and traditional souvenirs, especially as they are inexpensive.

A bottle of vodka, a jar of caviare, and packets of Soviet tea also make good souvenirs.

A Soviet camera is a splendid gift. Moscow stores have a wide range of good cameras at reasonable prices. Soviet watches, too, known for their reliability and precision, also make excellent keepsakes.

If you are a music lover you will not go wrong in buying records of Russian folk and classical music. Last but not least, there is the balalaika, which has gained recognition in the concert halls of many countries.

We recommend you do your souvenir buying at the kiosk in your hotel or the Russian Souvenir shop at No. 9 Kutuzov Prospekt.

Here is a list of other shops for your gift and souvenir hunting:

Art Shops	6 Ukrainsky Boulevard 46 Ulitsa Gorkogo (Gorky St.) 9 Kutuzov Prospekt 12 Ulitsa Petrovka
Books	Dom Knigi (The House of Books), 26 Prospekt Kalinina
	Druzhba (Friendship), 15 Ulitsa Gorkogo (Gorky St.) (books from socialist countries)
	Moskva, 8 Ulitsa Gorkogo
	Knizhnaya Lavka Pisatelei (The Writers' Bookstall), 18 Kuznetsky Most
	Inostrannaya Kniga (Books in Foreign Languages), 18 Kuznetsky Most
	Svetoch, 1/2 Ulitsa Solyanka
	Second-Hand Foreign Books, 16 Ulitsa Kachalova
Cameras and Photographic Supplies	**Jupiter, 27 Prospekt Kalinina** 25 Ulitsa Gorkogo (Gorky St.) 15 Ulitsa Petrovka 44 Komsomolsky Prospekt

Cut Glass	Khrustal (Crystal), 15 Ulitsa Gorkogo (Gorky St.) 8/2 Ulitsa Kirova
Gifts	Podarki (Gifts), 4 Ulitsa Gorkogo (Gorky St.) Podarki, 29 Prospekt Kalinina 9 Kutuzov Prospekt 6 Ukrainsky Boulevard
Jewellery	Malakhitovaya Shkatulka (The Malachite Casket), 24 Prospekt Kalinina 12 Ulitsa Gorkogo (Gorky St.) 9 Kutuzov Prospekt
Music	14 Ulitsa Neglinnaya 15 Ulitsa Gorkogo (Gorky St.) 13 Ulitsa Gertsena
Perfumery and Cosmetics	Seeren (Lilacs) 44 Prospekt Kalinina 8 Ulitsa Gorkogo (Gorky St.)
Records	Melodia, 40 Prospekt Kalinina
Stamps and Stamp Catalogues	31/22 Ulitsa Chekhova 92 Leninsky Prospekt 59 Prospekt Vernadskogo
Toys	Dom Igrushki (The House of Toys), 8 Kutuzov Prospekt
Wines and Spirits	4 Ulitsa Gorkogo (Gorky St.) 19 Kutuzov Prospekt 7 Stoleshnikov Pereulok
Miscellaneous	GUM (State Department Store), 3 Red Square TsUM (Central Department Store), 22 Ulitsa Petrovka Moskva, 56 Leninsky Prospekt Detsky Mir (Children's World), 2 Prospekt Marxa Moskvichka (Miss Moscow), 23 Prospekt Kalinina (ladies' fashions, haberdashery, lingerie, etc.) Sintetika, 27 Prospekt Kalinina

There are foreign-currency Beriozka shops in the following hotels: the Metropole, National, Berlin, Rossia, Ukraine, and Leningradskaya. In addition there is a special Beriozka shop at 9 Kutuzov Prospekt. In these shops you can buy furs, knitted goods, cut glass, porcelain, amber, watches, and many other articles.

NATIONAL DISHES OF THE USSR

When you are in Moscow, don't miss the chance to sample the variety of Russian cooking, which you can do quite easily by going to the restaurants in the Rossia and Tsentralnaya hotels or to the Slavyansky Bazar restaurant.

Russian snacks and appetisers—salads, cold fish, and aspics—are well known. Dishes we recommend are herring à la russe, salmon, sturgeon, jellied pike-perch, tongue, and *studen* (meat jelly). Caviare hardly needs advertising; but try it on buttered rye bread.

As for the soup course, such stand-byes as *borsch, shchi,* and *solyanka* are worth sampling. You might try *borsch* with mushrooms, Russian noodle soup, or *rassolnik* (pickled cucumber soup) with fish balls. In the summer Russians are very fond of cold vegetable or meat *okroshka* (kvass soup) and cold borsch.

Your impression of Russian cuisine will not be complete without tasting Siberian *pelmeni* (meat dumplings, rather like ravioli), with butter or sour cream, in bouillon or fried. You might also try *bliny* (Russian pancakes, usually served with caviare), *oladi* (raised pancakes), and *blinchiki* (fritters) with meat, cottage cheese, or apples.

Russians are very fond of cereals, especially buckwheat and semolina pudding. They are very nutritious and tasty with milk or butter. Some prefer them with sugar or jam.

You probably already know Russian vodka. There are various brands, we recommend *Extra* and *Starka.* But if you are feeling thirsty try a glass of Russian kvass.

Russian cuisine, of course, is only part of Soviet cuisine, which includes many dishes of all the nationalities that live in the USSR. Equally delicious are Russian meat pies, Ukrainian *borsch,* Uzbek *pilau,* Georgian *shashlyk,* Azerbaijan *piti,* and many other superb national dishes and snacks.

On the whole, Soviet cuisine does not differ much from European, especially in restaurants of hotels catering for foreign tourists.

But Moscow has many national restaurants where chefs prepare a wide range of delicacies. The **Aragvi** is one of the best of these. It serves around thirty of the main Georgian dishes, including *shashlyk,* chicken *satsivi,* grilled sturgeon, *suluguni* cheese, and chicken *tabaka.* The table wines of sunny Georgia are served. Among them are *Tsinandali* and *Gurdjaani* (white), *Mukuzani* (dry red), and *Kakhetinskoye* (white and red).

People who like eastern cuisine will enjoy the **Uzbekistan** and **Baku** restaurants.

A feature at the **Uzbekistan** is *tkhum-dulma* (hard-boiled egg in a fried meat patty), *mstava* (a rice soup with specially prepared meat), *lagman* (a spiced soup with meat and noodles) and aromatic Uzbek *pilau.* But the tastiest dish of all is probably *maniar*—a spiced broth, with minced meat, egg, and bits of pastry.

There is also a wide choice of main dishes in Uzbek cuisine, prepared from game, meat and vegetables. Their *shashlyks* are very tasty: they consist of small pieces of marinated meat grilled over charcoal.

The bread deserves mention; it is baked on the premises, in a special oven, Uzbek style. The temperature must be exactly 275 °C.

The best Uzbek dessert wines are *Aleatiko* and *Uzbekiston.*

The **Baku** is an Azerbaijan restaurant famous for its choice of pilaus. You may order pilau with chicken, mutton or beef, milk or eggs; and there are many sweet pilaus.

The soups are also delicious. *Piti*, for example, is prepared and served in a clay pot. Or you may try *dovta*, a sour milk soup with meat. Or a nut soup with chicken. The restaurant is also known for its *shashlyk*, *basturma*, *golubtsy* (chopped meat and rice in grape leaves), broiled chicken, to mention a few. Two excellent red Azerbaijan wines are *Medrese* and *Shamkhor*; *Aketafa* is a delicious dessert wine.

The **Ararat**, an Armenian restaurant, has an equally diversified menu of some 40 Armenian specialities. We recommend Armenian style *solyanka*, Yerevan *bozbash*, steamed, fried or broiled trout, Ararat *shashlyk*, roast lamb and pilau with raisins. The restaurant serves delicious *chebureki* (meat pasties fried in deep fat).

Armenia is famed for its brandies. The best are *Yubileiny* (Jubilee), *Armenia*, *Yerevan*, and *Dvin*. Many people prefer "ordinary" three-star Armenian brandy. Armenian muscats are also very good. Armenian sherry has a delicate fruit bouquet with a slight nutty flavour. Of the dessert wines, *Aigeshat* is recommended.

Of the other restaurants specialising in national dishes, the **Ukraine** is interesting for its rich meaty Ukrainian *borsch*, *galushki*, and wines. The best are the Massandra wines (from the south coast of the Crimea) and the dessert wines, the rosé, white, and black muscats, and the tokay. *Krasny Kamen* (Red Stone) is a world-famous Crimean muskat. Its bouquet captures the delicate fragrance of alpine pastures.

If you would like to sample the delicacies of the national cuisines of other countries, you should visit the Prague, Sofia, Budapest, Warsaw, Berlin, Belgrade, Bucharest, Havana, and Peking restaurants (see p. 177).

CITY TRANSPORT

Metro (see pp. 148-149 and diagram on the fly-leaf). The single fare is five kopecks, which covers any distance and all transfers to other lines. All you have to do to get on to the platform is drop a 5-kopeck piece into the slot machine. If you have not got the right change, you can use the change machines in the entrance hall of every Metro station. Trains run from 6:00 to 1:00 a.m. (except for national holidays when they run to 2:00 a.m.).

Trolleybuses run from 6:00 to 1:00. The single fare (no transfers), regardless of distance, is four kopecks.

Buses run from 6:00 to 1:00. The single fare (no transfers), regardless of distance, is five kopecks.

Trams start at 5:30 and run until 1:00. The single fare (no transfers), regardless of distance, is three kopecks.

Note: Most city trams, trolleybuses, and buses work without conductors. Instead there are ticket machines where the passenger drops in the fare and tears off a ticket. So we recommend you to keep a supply of 1-, 2-, 3- and 5-kopeck pieces. Tickets can also be bought in advance from newspaper kiosks or from the driver.

Taxis are easily recognisable by the checkered band on both sides of the car, and a green light in the top right-hand corner of the windscreen. When the green light is burning, the taxi is free. There are some 250 taxi ranks in the city marked with a "T". You can order a taxi by phone from your hotel (we advise you to do this through the service bureau). And of course you can hail a taxi anywhere in the streets by raising your arm, but not near a taxi rank if there is a queue. The fare is registered on a taximeter. The rate is 20 kopecks per kilometre, plus a 20-kopeck service charge (regardless of the number of passengers).

Fixed-route taxis *(marshrutniye taxi).* There are many fixed-route taxis (mini-buses) which run between the main squares, main thoroughfares, railway stations, and other important points, at intervals of ten minutes. They have definite stops along their routes, but if they are not full, they will stop at any point to pick up passengers. The single fare, regardless of distance, is 15 kopecks per person.

POST, TELEGRAPH, AND TELEPHONE

Postal arrangements in the Soviet Union are much the same as anywhere else. A letter or postcard can be posted from Moscow to any part of the world. There is a post office in practically every hotel, where you can buy stamps and stationery.

In the building of the Intourist Hotel, 3 Gorky St., there is a post restante office, K-600, which you can use as a forwarding address. It is convenient to use this service as tourists and visitors do not always know their address in advance. The address is simple, just Moscow, K-600, and Post Office K-600 is open daily from 9:00 to 18:00.

POSTAGE RATES (IN KOPEKS)

	To the CMEA countries		To other countries	
	Letter	Postcard	Letter	Postcard
Ordinary mail	4	3	15	10
Air mail	6	4	32	27
Registered mail	10	9	45	40
Registered air mail	12	10	62	57

Telegrams can be sent to any city in the world. Express telegrams are charged at double the ordinary rate.

Telephone calls can easily be put through to most cities in Europe and America, and to Australia and a number of countries in Asia and Africa. You can book a call from your hotel room or from special trunk-call offices. The charge of a three-minute conversation with most European countries is between 2.00 and 4.50 rubles, with the USA 11 rubles, with Japan 10.50 rubles.

A REMINDER FOR PEDESTRIANS

Traffic in Moscow streets is heavy and fast, and at rush hours it is quite difficult to cross certain streets because of the number of vehicles. It is as well therefore, in order to avoid accidents, to know Moscow's main traffic regulations.

Here are some of the basic rules:

—walk only on the pavements and keep to the right;

—cross streets only at pedestrian crossings, on the green "cross" sign;

—remember that Moscow drives on the right side of the road. Before crossing, look left and then, when you have reached the middle, look right;

—if you get caught by oncoming traffic when you are crossing, stand still to make it easier for drivers to go round you;

—only pass behind stationary buses and trolleybuses, but in front of stationary trams, otherwise you may not notice oncoming traffic;

—remember that it is prohibited for drivers to blow their horns in the city;

—remember that some streets have one-way traffic only;

—even when you are crossing a street at the green light, watch out for traffic coming from the left and turning right.

It is useful to remember that the house numbers on streets radiating from the Kremlin, as with all radial roads in Moscow, have even numbers on the right and odd numbers on the left, and begin the numbering from the centre.

SOME HINTS FOR MOTORISTS

Here are a few suggestions to help you drive confidently through Moscow's streets and squares, observing the city's traffic regulations.

As you already know, Moscow drives on the right side of the road. Remember, too, not to drive if you have had a drink.

Please also remember:

—to drive at a speed that ensures your own safety, and that of pedestrians. The speed limit in Moscow is 60 kilometres an hour (about 35 m.p.h.);

—horns and hooters may only be used outside the city limits, or in an emergency to prevent an accident;

—listen for the sirens of special service vehicles (fire engines, ambulances, etc.) and give way to them;

—reduce speed before crossroads and zebra crossings.

CAR INSURANCE

If you did not insure your car at the Soviet border, you may do so in Moscow at the offices of **Ingosstrakh** (the Foreign Insurance Agency), 11 Kuibyshev Street. This organisation insures all forms of transport, against third party risks (person and property) and accidents on the territory of the USSR. Policies are made out in any currency. Premiums are payable and claims are met in the currency used in making out the policy.

AN ABC OF MOSCOW'S MAIN STREETS AND THOROUGHFARES

To help the motorist find his way through Moscow streets, here is a concise list of the city's main thoroughfares.

The ring roads are lettered: Boulevard Ring being *A*, Sadovoye Ring is *Б*, the inner circular thoroughfare (Begovaya St.—Nizhnyaya Maslovka St.—Sushchovsky Val) is *B*, and the outer Circular Road is *K*.

The avenues and major streets radiating from the centre are numbered. The letter *M* is added to the number of a radial street if it is a continuation of a major motor road. For instance, the road to Leningrad is No. 10. Within Moscow it becomes Leningrad Highway, then Leningrad Prospekt, which is therefore numbered M10.

Here is a list of Moscow's radial highways and their destinations:

M1—Kutuzov Prospekt, Minsk Highway—to Smolensk, Minsk, and Brest

M4—Warsaw Highway—to Kharkov, Simferopol, and Yalta

M8—Entuziasty Highway—to Vladimir and Suzdal

M9—Mir Prospekt, Yaroslavl Highway—to Zagorsk and Yaroslavl

M10—Leningrad Prospekt, Leningrad Highway—to Leningrad.

FOR FACT COLLECTORS

—in Moscow there are 100,000 Ivanovs and over 100,000 Kuznetsovs, which are the two most common surnames in Moscow;

—at the time of the latest census there were 113 Muscovites over 100 years old;

—every day Moscow's theatres and concert halls are attended by more than 45,000 people, and the cinemas by 300,000;

—every day Muscovites receive and send over three million letters and postcards;

—there are 8,000 amateur art and drama groups in Moscow, including 1,000 choirs, 2,150 musical ensembles and 715 dance groups;

—Moscow Region has 20 sanatoriums and over 60 holiday homes belonging to the trade unions, and a large number of other ones run by various institutions, together accommodating over 800,000 people;

—there are over 70 camping sites for short holidays in the Green Belt one to two hours' drive from the city;

—there are over a hundred excursion boats and motor launches in Moscow and more than 800,000 people take trips on the river and the Moscow Canal every summer;

—the city has 100 parks and over 600 public gardens;

—in winter the skating rinks in Moscow parks cover more than 250,000 square metres;

—in order to clear the streets and squares of the city of snow ten centimetres thick, dump trucks must make 150,000 journeys;

—the Moskva River has over 600 tributaries, and is spanned by 15 bridges; there are over 200 bridges (including flyovers) in Moscow;

—in the past Moscow often suffered from flooding; in 1908 the Moskva River rose nine metres and flooded 100 streets and 2,500 houses; the city is no longer threatened by flooding;

—there are swans (including the black Australian variety) on 14 lakes in Moscow, and wild geese and ducks; sparrows and pigeons are the most common birds in Moscow;

—in 1932 there were 40,000 horses in the city; now there are only around 650, mostly at the Race Course and the five riding schools;

—Muscovites own 65,000 dogs, 250,000 cats, and tens of thousands of cage birds;

—there are more than 8,000 elks in the woods of Moscow's Green Belt;

—there are 114 varieties of tree and shrub in Moscow streets, squares, boulevards, and courtyards, including pines, birches, poplars, limes, oaks, and maples;

—in Kolomenskoye there are 400-year-old oaks, and a few 600-year-old ones;

—Muscovites (and visitors) are very fond of ice-cream, eating more than 170 tons a day winter and summer alike;

—there are around 7,800 cafeterias, cafés, restaurants, buffets, bars, and other eating places in Moscow;

—Moscow city transport carries around 15 million passengers a day on the Metro and several thousand buses, over 2,000 trolleybuses and more than 16,000 taxis.

ADDRESSES OF MUSEUMS, EXHIBITIONS, THEATRES, CINEMAS, CONCERT HALLS, CIRCUSES, PARKS, SPORTS FACILITIES, HOTELS, RESTAURANTS AND MARKETS

MUSEUMS OF THE HISTORY OF THE REVOLUTION

Central Lenin Museum (see pp. 82, 83)—2 Ploshchad Revolutsii
Karl Marx and Frederick Engels Museum (see p. 100, 101)—5 Ulitsa Marxa i Engelsa
Museum of the Revolution (see p. 74, 75)—21 Ulitsa Gorkogo (Gorky Street)
Kalinin Museum (see p. 97)—21 Prospekt Marxa

HISTORY MUSEUMS

History Museum (see pp. 43, 44)—Red Square
Branches: Novodevichy Convent (see pp. 22, 43, 104, 135, 150)—
           1 Novodevichy Proyezd
           St. Basil's Cathedral (Cathedral of the Intercession) (see pp. 40, 41)—Red Square

Museum of the History and Reconstruction of Moscow (see p. 87)—12 Novaya Ploshchad
Central Museum of the USSR Armed Forces—2 Ploshchad Kommuny
Battle of Borodino Panorama and Museum (see pp. 116, 117)—38 Kutuzovsky Prospekt

ART MUSEUMS

Tretyakov Art Gallery (see pp. 60, 97, 99, 100)—10 Lavrushinsky Pereulok
Pushkin Museum of Fine Arts (see pp. 100, 101)—12 Volkhonka Ulitsa
Museum of Folk Art—7 Ulitsa Stanislavskogo
Museum of Oriental Art—16 Ulitsa Obukha
Ostankino Palace and Museum of Serf Art (see pp. 127, 128)—5 Pervaya Ostankinskaya Ulitsa
Rublev Museum of Early Russian Art (former Andronikov Monastery)—10 Ploshchad Pryamikova
Museum of the Moscow Kremlin—The Kremlin

LITERARY MUSEUMS

Gorky Memorial Museum—6 Ulitsa Kachalova
Tolstoy Museum (see p. 104)—11 Kropotkinskaya Ulitsa
Tolstoy Mansion (see p. 104)—21 Ulitsa Lva Tolstogo
Pushkin Museum—12 Kropotkinskaya Ulitsa
Chekhov Museum—6 Sadovaya-Kudrinskaya Ulitsa
Dostoyevsky Museum—2 Ulitsa Dostoyevskogo
Mayakovsky Museum (see p. 87)—3 Proyezd Serova
Nikolai Ostrovsky Museum (see p. 84)—14 Ulitsa Gorkogo (Gorky Street)

THEATRICAL AND MUSIC MUSEUMS

Bakhrushin Theatrical Museum—31/12 Ulitsa Bakhrushina
Stanislavsky Museum—6 Ulitsa Stanislavskogo
Glinka Central Music Museum—4 Ulitsa Fadeyeva
Skryabin Museum—11 Ulitsa Vakhtangova

SCIENCE AND POLYTECHNICAL MUSEUMS AND BOTANICAL GARDENS

Polytechnical Museum (see p. 87)—3/4 Novaya Ploshchad
Planetarium—5 Sadovaya-Kudrinskaya Ulitsa
Zoological Museum—6 Ulitsa Gertsena
Main Botanical Gardens of the USSR Academy of Sciences—4 Botanicheskaya Ulitsa
Zoo—1 Bolshaya Gruzinskaya Ulitsa

EXHIBITIONS AND EXHIBITION HALLS

USSR Economic Exhibition (VDNKh) (see pp. 119, 127)—Prospekt Mira (VDNKh Metro station)
Building Section of USSR Economic Exhibition—30 Frunzenskaya Naberezhnaya
Children's Book Exhibition (see p. 71)—43 Ulitsa Gorkogo (Gorky Street)
House of Fashions (see p. 91)—14 Kuznetsky Most
Central Exhibition Hall (see p. 95)—1 Ploshchad Pyatidesyatiletia Oktyabrya
Exhibition Halls of the USSR and RSFSR Unions of Artists (see p. 91): 11 Kuznetsky Most; 20 Kuznetsky Most; 46b Ulitsa Gorkogo (Gorky Street); 7/9 Begovaya Ulitsa

THEATRES, CONCERT HALLS AND CIRCUSES

Palace of Congresses (see pp. 53, 54, 64)—The Kremlin
Bolshoi Theatre (see pp. 87, 90)—2 Ploshchad Sverdlova
Maly Theatre (see p. 99)—1/6 Ploshchad Sverdlova Branch—69 Bolshaya Ordynka
Moscow Art Theatre (see p. 88)—3 Proyezd Khudozhestvennogo Teatra
    New building—24 Tverskoi Boulevard
    Branch—3 Ulitsa Moskvina
Vakhtangov Theatre—26 Arbat
Mossoviet Theatre (see p. 79)—16 Bolshaya Sadovaya Ulitsa
Stanislavsky and Nemirovich-Danchenko Musical Theatre—17 Pushkinskaya Ulitsa
Mayakovsky Theatre—19 Ulitsa Gertsena
Central Theatre of the Soviet Army—Ploshchad Kommuny
Lenin Komsomol Theatre—6 Ulitsa Chekhova
Pushkin Drama Theatre—23 Tverskoi Boulevard
Satire Theatre (see p. 71)—18 Bolshaya Sadovaya Ulitsa
Yermolova Theatre (see p. 80)—5 Ulitsa Gorkogo (Gorky Street)
Operetta Theatre—6 Pushkinskaya Ulitsa
Stanislavsky Drama Theatre (see p. 73)—23 Ulitsa Gorkogo (Gorky Street)
Gogol Drama Theatre—8 Ulitsa Kazakova
Sovremennik Theatre—19 Chistiye Prudy
Taganka Theatre—76 Ulitsa Chkalova
Malaya Bronnaya Theatre—2 Malaya Bronnaya Ulitsa
Romany Gipsy Theatre (see p. 67)—38 Leningradsky Prospekt
Central Puppet Theatre (directed by Sergei Obraztsov)—3 Sadovaya-Samotyochnaya Ulitsa
Central Children's Theatre (see p. 91)—7/2 Ploshchad Sverdlova
Young Spectators' Theatre (see p. 73)—10 Pereulok Sadovskikh
Moscow Puppet Theatre—26 Spartakovskaya Ulitsa
Children's Musical Theatre—17 Ulitsa Dvadtsat Pyatogo Oktyabrya
Variety Theatre—20 Bersenevskaya Naberezhnaya
Theatre of Miniatures—3 Karetny Ryad
Television Theatre—1 Ploshchad Zhuravlyova
Film Actors' Studio Theatre—33 Ulitsa Vorovskogo
Circus (new) (see p. 132)—17 Prospekt Vernadskogo
Circus (old)—13 Tsvetnoi Boulevard
Rossia Concert Hall (see p. 43)—Rossia Hotel, 1 Moskvoretskaya Naberezhnaya
Tchaikovsky Concert Hall (see p. 79)—31 Ulitsa Gorkogo (Gorky Street)
Moscow Conservatoire (see p. 95)—13 Ulitsa Gertsena
House of Trade Unions (Dom Soyuzov), Hall of Columns and October Hall—1 Pushkinskaya
    Ulitsa
Concert Hall of the Central Art Workers Club—9 Pushechnaya Ulitsa
Oktyabr Cinema-Concert Hall (see p. 111)—42 Prospekt Kalinina
Warsaw Cinema-Concert Hall—10 Leningradskoye Shosse

CINEMAS

Circorama (see p. 126)—Prospekt Mira, in the grounds of the USSR Economic Exhibition
Cosmos (see p. 122)—109 Prospekt Mira
Gorizont—21 Komsomolsky Prospekt
Khudozhestvenny (see p. 109)—14 Arbatskaya Ploshchad
Metropole (see p. 86)—1 Prospekt Marxa
Mir—11 Tsvetnoi Boulevard
Moskva—2 Ploshchad Mayakovskogo
Oktyabr (see p. 111)—42 Prospekt Kalinina
Rossia (see p. 76)—Pushkinskaya Ploshchad
Udarnik—2 Ulitsa Serafimovicha
Zaryadye (see p. 43)—Rossia Hotel, 1 Moskvoretskaya Naberezhnaya

PARKS AND GARDENS

Gorky Central Park (see pp. 133)—9 Krymsky Val
Izmailovo Park—17 Narodny Prospekt
Sokolniki Park—62 Rusakovskaya Ulitsa
Dzerzhinsky Park (see p. 127)—7 Pervaya Ostankinskaya Ulitsa
Krasnaya Presnya Park—5 Mantulinskaya Ulitsa
Gardens of the Central Club of the Soviet Army—2 Ploshchad Kommuny
Hermitage Gardens—3 Karetny Ryad
Aquarium Gardens—16 Bolshaya Sadovaya Ulitsa

STADIUMS AND SPORTS FACILITIES

Lenin Central Stadium (see pp. 26, 104, 135, 139)—Luzhniki
Dynamo Stadium (see p. 70)—36 Leningradsky Prospekt
Lokomotiv Central Stadium—125 Bolshaya Cherkizovskaya Ulitsa

Central Army Sports Club Stadium (see p. 70)–39 Leningradsky Prospekt
Young Pioneers' Stadium and Cycle Track (see p. 70)–31 Leningradsky Prospekt
Race Course (see p. 67)–22 Begovaya Ulitsa
Water Sports Palace–27 Mironovskaya Ulitsa
Moskva Swimming Pool (see pp. 26, 104)–37 Kropotkinskaya Naberezhnaya
Chaika Swimming Pool–1 Turchaninov Pereulok

HOTELS

Hotel   Address   nearest Metro stations
Aeroflot (see p. 70)–37 Leningradsky Prospekt, *Dinamo, Aeroport*
Altai–12 Gostinichnaya Ulitsa, *VDNKh*
Armenia–4 Neglinnaya Ulitsa, *Prospekt Marxa, Dzerzhinskaya*
Belgrade*–5 and 6 Smolenskaya Ulitsa, *Smolenskaya*
Berlin*–3 Ulitsa Zhdanova, *Dzerzhinskaya*
Bucharest–1 Sadovnicheskaya Naberezhnaya, *Novokuznetskaya*
Budapest–2 Petrovskiye Linii, *Prospekt Marxa, Ploshchad Sverdlova, Kuznetsky Most*
Tsentralnaya (see p. 76)–10 Ulitsa Gorkogo (Gorky Street), *Pushkinskaya, Prospekt Marxa*
Intourist* (see p. 80)–3 Ulitsa Gorkogo (Gorky Street), *Prospekt Marxa*
Kievskaya–2/16 Kievskaya Ulitsa, *Kievskaya*
Leningradskaya–21 Kalanchovskaya Ulitsa, *Komsomolskaya*
Metropole* (see p. 86)–1 Prospekt Marxa, *Ploshchad Sverdlova, Ploshchad Revolutsii, Prospekt Marxa*
Minsk (see p. 71)–22 Ulitsa Gorkogo (Gorky Street), *Mayakovskaya, Pushkinskaya*
Mir–9 Bolshoi Devyatinsky Pereulok, *Krasnopresnenskaya*
Moskva (see p. 92)–7 Prospekt Marxa, *Prospekt Marxa, Ploshchad Sverdlova, Ploshchad Revolutsii*
Mozhaiskaya (motel)–Minskoye Shosse (junction of the Moscow Road)
National* (see p. 92)–14 Prospekt Marxa, *Prospekt Marxa*
Ostankino–29 Botanicheskaya Ulitsa, *VDNKh*
Peking (see p. 71)–1 Bolshaya Sadovaya Ulitas, *Mayakovskaya*
Rossia (see pp. 42, 43)–6 Ulitsa Razina, *Ploshchad Nogina, Ploshchad Revolutsii*
Severnaya–50 Sushchovsky Val, *Novoslobodskaya*
Sovetskaya (see p. 67)–32 Leningradsky Prospekt, *Dinamo*
Sport–Lenin Central Stadium, Luzhniki, *Sportivnaya, Leninskiye Gory*
Sputnik–38 Leninsky Prospekt, *Leninsky Prospekt*
Tourist–17 Selskokhozyaistvennaya Ulitsa, *VDNKh*
Ukraine (see p. 113)–2 Kutuzovsky Prospekt, *Kievskaya*
Urals–40 Ulitsa Chernyshevskogo, *Ploshchad Nogina, Kirovskaya, Kurskaya*
Vostok–8 Gostinichny Proyezd, *VDNKh*
Warsaw–2 Oktyabrskaya Ploshchad, *Oktyabrskaya*
Yunost–34 Frunzensky Val, *Sportivnaya*
Yaroslavskaya–8 Yaroslavskaya Ulitsa, *VDNKh*

Zarya–5 Gostinichnaya Ulitsa, *VDNKh*
Zolotoi Kolos–15 Yaroslavskaya Ulitsa, *VDNKh*
Hotels marked (*) belong to Intourist.

RESTAURANTS

Aragvi (Georgian cuisine) (see p. 79, 164)–6 Ulitsa Gorkogo (Gorky Street)
Ararat (Armenian cuisine) (see p. 165)–4 Neglinnaya Ulitsa
Arbat (see p. 111)–29 Prospekt Kalinina
Baku (Azerbaijanian cuisine) (see p. 164)–24 Ulitsa Gorkogo (Gorky Street)
Belgrade (see p. 165)–5 and 6 Smolenskaya Ulitsa
Berlin (see p. 165)–6 Pushechnaya Ulitsa
Bucharest (see p. 165)–1 Sadovnicheskaya Naberezhnaya
Budapest (see p. 165)–2 Petrovskiye Linii
Havana–88 Leninsky Prospekt
Intourist (see p. 80)–3 Ulitsa Gorkogo (Gorky Street)
Metropole (see p. 86)–1 Prospekt Marxa
Minsk (Byelorussian cuisine) (see p. 71)–22 Ulitsa Gorkogo (Gorky Street)
Moskva (see p. 92)–7 Prospekt Marxa
National (see p. 92)–1 Ulitsa Gorkogo (Gorky Street)
Peking (see p. 165)–1 Bolshaya Sadovaya Ulitsa
Prague (see p. 165)–2 Ulitsa Arbat
Rossia (Russian cuisine) (see pp. 42, 43)–6 Ulitsa Razina
Slavyansky Bazar (Russian cuisine)–17 Ulitsa Dvadtsat Pyatogo Oktyabrya
Sofia (see p. 71)–32 Ulitsa Gorkogo (Gorky Street)
Tsentralny (Russian cuisine) (see p. 76)–10 Ulitsa Gorkogo (Gorky Street)
Ukraine (Ukrainian cuisine) (see p. 165)–2 Kutuzovsky Prospekt
Uzbekistan (Uzbek cuisine) (see p. 164)–29 Neglinnaya Ulitsa
Volga (see p. 70)–89 Leningradskoye Shosse (Northern Port)
Warsaw (see p. 165)–2 Krymsky Val
Zolotoi Kolos (see p. 126)–Prospekt Mira, on the grounds of the USSR Economic Exhibition
Zvezdnoye Nebo–Intourist Hotel, 3 Ulitsa Gorkogo (Gorky Street)

MARKETS

Tsentralny–15 Tsvetnoi Boulevard
Leningradsky–11 Chasovaya Ulitsa
Cheryomushkinsky–1/42 Lomonosovsky Prospekt

SOME OTHER USEFUL ADDRESSES

Executive Committee of the Moscow City Soviet People's Deputies—13 Ulitsa Gorkogo (Gorky Street)

USSR Ministry of Foreign Affairs—32/34 Smolenskaya-Sennaya Ploshchad

Soviet Friendship Societies for Cultural Relations with Foreign Countries—14 Prospekt Kalinina

All-Union Chamber of Trade and Commerce—6 Ulitsa Kuibysheva

Soviet Peace Committee (see p. 104)—10 Kropotkinskaya Ulitsa

Soviet Women's Committee—23 Pushkinskaya Ulitsa

USSR Committee of Youth Organisations—7/8 Ulitsa Bogdana Khmelnitskogo

Soviet Peace Fund—10 Kropotkinskaya Ulitsa

Soviet Committee for Cultural Relations with Compatriots Abroad—10 Bolshoi Kharitonyevsky Pereulok

Union of Red Cross and Red Crescent Societies—5 Pervy Cheryomushkinsky Proyezd

Soviet War Veterans' Committee (see p. 104)—4 Gogolevsky Boulevard

Soviet European Security Committee—3 Kropotkinskaya Ulitsa

Soviet Afro-Asian Solidarity Committee (see p. 104)—10 Kropotkinskaya Ulitsa

USSR Znaniye (Knowledge) Society—4 Proyezd Serova

Committee for Physical Culture and Sport of the USSR Council of Ministers—4 Skatertny Pereulok

Organising Committee for the 1980 Olympic Games—22a Ulitsa Gorkogo (Gorky Street)

All-Union Central Council of Trade Unions—42 Leninsky Prospekt

USSR United Nations Association—19 Ulitsa Dmitriya Ulyanova

Friendship House—16 Prospekt Kalinina

USSR Union of Architects—3 Ulitsa Shchuseva

USSR Union of Journalists—8 Suvorovsky Boulevard

USSR Union of Composers—8/10 Ulitsa Nezhdanovoi

USSR Union of Writers—52 Ulitsa Vorovskogo

USSR Union of Film Workers—13 Vasilievskaya Ulitsa

USSR Union of Artists—10 Gogolevsky Boulevard

All-Russia Theatrical Society (see p. 76)—16/2 Ulitsa Gorkogo (Gorky Street)

USSR Bank of Foreign Trade (Vneshtorgbank)—12 Neglinnaya Ulitsa, Korpus B

USSR State Bank—12 Neglinnaya Ulitsa

Central Board of Foreign Tourism of the USSR Council of Ministers (see p. 94)—16 Prospekt Marxa

Ingosstrakh (USSR Insurance Company)—11 Ulitsa Kuibysheva

Intourist Board (see p. 86)—16 Prospekt Marxa

Intourist Travel Agency—1 Ploshchad Sverdlova

Intourist Excursion Bureau—1 Ulitsa Gorkogo (Gorky Street)

Sputnik International Youth Travel Agency (see p. 191)—15 Vorobyovskoye Shosse

Central Telegraph Office (see p. 80)—7 Ulitsa Gorkogo (Gorky Street)

International Telephone Exchange (see p. 88)—7 Ulitsa Gorkogo (Gorky Street), entrance 10 at
   Ulitsa Ogareva
Central Post Office—26 Ulitsa Kirova

PRESS, RADIO, TELEVISION
AND NEWS AGENCIES

NEWSPAPERS

Pravda—24 Ulitsa Pravdy
Izvestia—5 Pushkinskaya Ploshchad
Trud—18b Ulitsa Gorkogo (Gorky Street)
Sotsialisticheskaya Industriya—73 Novoslobodskaya Ulitsa
Komsomolskaya Pravda—24 Ulitsa Pravdy
Sovetskaya Kultura—73 Novoslobodskaya Ulitsa
Sovetsky Sport—8 Ulitsa Arkhipova
Literaturnaya Gazeta—30 Tsvetnoi Boulevard
Sovetskaya Rossia—24 Ulitsa Pravdy
Moskovskaya Pravda—7 Ulitsa Devyatsot Pyatogo Goda
Vechernyaya Moskva—7 Ulitsa Devyatsot Pyatogo Goda
Moscow News (and associated newspapers) (see p. 76)—2 Pushkinskaya Ploshchad
Neues Leben—14 Bumazhny Proyezd

MAGAZINES

Kommunist–5 Ulitsa Marxa i Engelsa
Soviet Union–8 Ulitsa Moskvina
Vneshnyaya Torgovlya (Foreign Trade)–4 Ulitsa Pudovkina
Inostrannaya Literatura–41 Pyatnitskaya Ulitsa
International Affairs–14 Gorokhovsky Pereulok
New Times–1/2 Maly Putinkovsky Pereulok
Novy Mir–1/2 Maly Putinkovsky Pereulok
Ogonyok–14 Bumazhny Proyezd
Rabotnitsa–14 Bumazhny Proyezd
Soviet Woman–22 Kuznetsky Most
Soviet Literature–7 Naberezhnaya Shevchenko
Tourist–14 Bolshoi Kharitonyevsky Pereulok
Travel to the USSR–8 Neglinnaya Ulitsa

TASS (USSR Telegraph Agency)–10 Tverskoi Boulevard
Novosti Press Agency (APN)–2 Maly Putinkovsky Pereulok
USSR State Committee for Television and Radio Broadcasting–25 Pyatnitskaya Ulitsa
USSR State Committee for Publishing, Printing, and the Book Trade–26 Ulitsa Petrovka

TELEPHONE NUMBERS TO REMEMBER

01–Fire
02–Police
03–Ambulance
09–Directory inquiries (in Russian)
100–Time

INDEX OF
NAMES AND PLACES

A SHORT PHRASE-BOOK

GUIDE TO PRONOUNCIATION

	Symbol	Approximate pronunciation	Example
Vowels	a	as a in comma	kar'teena
	ah	as ah in shah	'sahkhar
	e	as e in penny	gdje, rad'noje
	ee	as ee in seeking	kar'teena
	i	as i in sister	vi
	o	as o in sore	shto
	u	as u in bull	chugun
Consonants	j	as y in yeast	i'julj
	g	as g in guide	gerp, girja
	s	as s in sister	bees
	ch	as ch in cheese	doch
	kh	as ch in Scottish loch	'sahkhar, dukh
	sh	as sh in shah	shahpka
	zh	as s in measure	zhizn

The other symbols used here (**b, d, f, k, l, m, n, p, r, t, v, z**) are pronounced similar to their English counterparts.

ARRIVAL

Носильщик!	Na'seelshik!	Porter!
Скажите, пожалуйста, где стоянка такси?	Ska'zhiti, pa'zhahlsta, 'gdje sta'jahnka tak'see?	Where can I get a taxi, please?
Где представитель (отделение) „Интуриста"?	'Gdje pritsta'veetil (addi'lenje) intu'reesta?	Where is the Intourist representative (office)?
Как проехать в гостиницу . . . ?	'Khak pra'jekhat vga'steenitsu . . . ?	Where is the . . . hotel?
Я иностранец (m) /иностранка (f).	'Jah ina'strahnits /ina'strahnka.	I am a foreigner
Я турист.	'Jah tu'reest.	I am a tourist

187

CUSTOMS

У меня нет ничего, что подлежит пошлинной оплате.	U mi'njah 'njet nichi'vo, shto padli'zhit 'poshlinnaj a'plahti.	I have nothing to declare
Это вещи личного пользования.	'Eto 'veshchi 'leechnava 'poljzavanja	These things are for personal use
Вот моя валюта.	'Vot ma'jah va'ljuta.	Here is my money
Весь этот багаж мой.	'Vjes 'etat ba'gahsh 'moj.	This is all my baggage
Где будет таможенное оформление?	'Gdje 'budit ta'mozhinaje afarm'lenje?	Where do I pass through customs?
Это мой (чужой) чемодан.	'Eta 'moj (chu'zhoj) chima'dahn.	This is my (someone else's) suitcase
Какую пошлину я должен уплатить?	Ka'kuju 'poshlinu ja 'dolzhin upla'teet?	How much duty must I pay?
Досмотр окончен?	Da'smotr a'konchin?	Is the inspection finished?
Есть ли лишний вес?	'Jest li 'leeshnij 'vjes?	Is my baggage overweight?
Сколько я должен уплатить за лишний вес?	'Skolka ja 'dolzhin upla'teet za 'leeshnij 'vjes?	How much must I pay for overweight baggage?

HOTEL ACCOMMODATION

Мне нужен номер для одного человека, с ванной (душем).	'Mnje 'nuzhin 'nomir dlja adna'vo chila'vjeka, 'svahnnaj ('zdushim).	I want a single room with bath (shower)
Нам с женой нужен один номер на двоих.	'Nahmz zhi'noj 'nuzhin a'deen 'nomir na dva'eekh.	My wife and I would like a double room
Дайте мне, пожалуйста, ключ от номера.	'Dajti mnje, pa'zhahlsta, 'kljuch at'nomira.	May I have the key to my room?
Доставьте, пожалуйста, мой багаж в номер.	Da'stahfti, pa'zhahlsta, moj ba'gashs v'nomir.	Please take my baggage to my room
Какой номер моей комнаты?	Ka'koj 'nomir ma'jej 'komnati?	What is my room number?
Где я могу позавтракать (пообедать, поужинать)?	'Gdje ja ma'gu pa'zahftrakat (pa-a'bjedat, pa'uzhinat)?	Where can I have breakfast (lunch, dinner)?
Где я могу купить иностранные газеты?	'Gdje ja ma'gu ku'peet ina'strahnnije ga'zeti?	Where can I buy foreign newspapers?
Разбудите меня, пожалуйста, в... часов ... минут.	Razbu'deeti mi'njah, pa'zhahlsta, v... chi'sof... mi'nut.	Please wake me at...
Где находится лифт (бюро обслуживания, ресторан, кафе)?	'Gdje na'khoditsa 'leeft (bju'ro aps'luzhivanja, rista'rahn, ka'fe)?	Where is the elevator (service bureau, restaurant, café)?
Я остановился в гостинице...	'Jah astana'veelsa vga'steenitsi...	I am staying at the ... hotel

Я живу в ... номере на ... этаже.	'Jah zhi'vu v ...'nomiri na ... ita'zhe.	I live in room ... on the ... floor
Одну минуту!	Ad'nu mi'nutu!	Wait a minute!
Войдите!	Vaj'deeti!	Come in
Можно ли здесь обменять валюту?	'Mozhna li zdjes abmi'njaht va'ljutu?	Can I change money here?
Где можно позвонить по телефону?	'Gdje 'mozhna pazva'neet pa tili'fonu?	Where can I make a phone call?
Купите, пожалуйста, мне билет (два билета) в театр на завтра, на спектакль ...	Ku'piti, pa'zhahlsta, 'mnje bi'ljet ('dvah bi'ljeta) f ti'ahtar na 'zahftra, na spik'tahkl ...	Please buy me a ticket (two tickets) to the theatre for tomorrow's performance of ...
Нет ли для меня корреспонденции?	'Njet li dlja mi'njah karispan'dentsii?	Is there any mail for me?

AT THE BANK

Где находится ближайший банк?	'Gdje na'khoditsa bli'zhajshij 'bahnk?	Where is the nearest bank?
Я хотел бы обменять валюту и один чек.	'Jah kha'tjel bi abmi'njaht va'ljutu i a'deen 'chek.	I should like to change money and one traveller's cheque
Какие требуются документы, чтобы обменять валюту?	Ka'keeje 'trebujutsa daku'mjenti, 'shtobi abmi'njaht va'ljutu?	What documents do I need to change money?
Разменяйте пожалуйста, десять (пять) рублей, три рубля.	Razmi'njajti, pa'zhahlsta, 'djesit ('pjaht) ru'blej, 'tree rub'ljah.	Can you change a ten-ruble (five-ruble, three-ruble) note?

MEETING PEOPLE

Здравствуйте!	'Zdrahstvujti!	Hello!
Доброе утро!	'Dobraje 'utra!	Good morning!
Добрый день!	'Dobrij 'djen!	Good afternoon!
Добрый вечер!	'Dobrij 'vechir!	Good evening!
До свиданья!	Dasvi'dahnja!	Goodbye!
Господин	Gaspa'deen	Mr.
Госпожа	Gaspa'zhah	Mrs./Miss/Ms.
Товарищ	Ta'varish	Comrade
Разрешите представиться, меня зовут ...	Razri'shiti prit'stahvitsa, mi'njah za'vut ...	Let me introduce myself My name is ...
Как вас зовут?	'Kahk vaz za'vut?	What's your name?
Сколько вам лет?	'Skolka vam 'ljet?	How old are you?
Я приехал из ...	'Jah pri'jekhal iz ...	I am from ...
Отец	A'tjets	Father
Мать	'Maht	Mother
Брат	'Braht	Brother
Сестра	Sis'trah	Sister

189

Сын	Sinn	Son
Дочь	Doch	Daughter
Мальчик	'Mahlchik	Boy
Девушка; девочка	'Djevushka; 'djevachka	Girl
Мужчина	Mush'cheena	Man
Женщина	'Zhenshina	Woman
Муж, супруг	'Mush, su'pruk	Husband, spouse
Жена, супруга	Zhi'nah, sup'ruga	Wife, spouse
Рабочий (m)/работница (f)	Ra'bochij/ra'botnitsa	Worker
Крестьянин/крестьянка	Kris'tjahnin/kris'tjahnka	Peasant
Служащий/служащая	'Sluzhashij/sluzhashija	Office or professional worker
Общественный деятель	Ap'shestvinij 'dejatil	Public figure
Журналист	Zhurna'leest	Journalist
Писатель	Pi'sahtil	Writer
Учитель/учительница	U'cheetil/u'cheetilnitsa	Teacher
Актер/актриса	Ak'tjor/ak'treesa	Actor/actress
Студент/студентка	Stu'djent/stu'djentka	Student
Инженер	Inzhi'njer	Engineer
Врач	Vrahch	Doctor
Шахтер	Shakh'tjor	Miner
Механик	Mi'khahnik	Mechanic
Художник	Khu'dozhnik	Artist
Переводчик	Piri'votchik	Interpreter
Группа	'Grupa	Group
Экскурсия	Iks'kursija	Excursion

SOME COMMON EXPRESSIONS

Позовите, пожалуйста, переводчика.	Paza'veeti, pa'zhahlsta, piri'votchika.	Please get an interpreter
Помогите, пожалуйста!	Pama'geeti, pa'zhahlsta.	Please help me!
Прошу вас проводить (встретить) меня...	Pra'shu prava'deet ('fstretit) mi'njah.	Please take me to ... (meet me at)...
Благодарю вас.	Blagada'rju vas.	I am very grateful to you
Спасибо.	Spa'seeba.	Thank you
Извините, пожалуйста.	Izvi'neeti, pa'zhahlsta.	Please forgive me
Простите.	Pra'steeti.	Excuse me
Я хочу отдохнуть (есть, пить, спать).	'Jah kha'chu addakh'nut ('jest, 'pjit, 'spaht).	I want to rest (eat, drink, sleep)
Я хочу осмотреть город (выставку, музей).	'Jah kha'chu asma'tret 'gorat ('vistavku, mu'zej).	I'd like to see the city (exhibition, museum)
Я хочу пойти в театр (в кино, в парк).	'Jah kha'chu paj'ti fti'ahtar (fki'no, 'fpark).	I'd like to go to the theatre (the cinema, a park)
Я хочу купить что-нибудь на память.	'Jah kha'chu ku'peet 'shtonibut na 'pahmit.	I want to buy a souvenir
Я согласен (m)/согласна (f).	'Jah sa'glahsin/sa'glahsna.	I agree
Не возражаю.	Ni vazra'zhaju.	I don't mind
Да, конечно.	'Dah, ka'njeshna.	Yes, of course
С удовольствием!	Suda'volstvijim.	With pleasure!

Я не хочу.	'Jah ni kha'chu	I don't want to
Я не могу.	'Jah ni ma'gu.	I can't
Нет, спасибо.	'Njet, spa'seeba.	No, thank you
К сожалению, я занят (m)/занята (f)	Ksazhi'lenju, 'jah 'zahnit/'zahnita.	Unfortunately, I am busy
Я не согласен (не согласна) с вами	'Jah ni sa'glahsin /ni sa'glahsna/s'vahmi.	I don't agree with you
Поздравляю вас!	Pazdrav'ljaju vas!	Congratulations!
За ваше здоровье!	Za 'vahshe zda'rovje!	To your health!
Желаю счастья (здоровья, успеха).	Zhi'laju 'shchahstja (zda'rovja, us'pjekhav).	I wish you happiness (good health, success)
Я не понимаю вас.	'Jah ni pani'maju vas.	I don't understand you
Я говорю (только) по-английски (по-французски, по-...).	'Jah gava'rju ('tolka) pa-angleejski (pa-fran'tsuski, pa-...).	I (only) speak English (French...)
Повторите, пожалуйста.	Pafta'reeti, pa'zhahlsta.	Please repeat what you said
Говорите, пожалуйста, медленнее.	Gava'reeti, pa'zhahlsta, 'mjedlinij.	Speak a little slower, please

DAYS OF THE WEEK, MONTHS, SEASONS

Какой сегодня день?	Ka'koi si'vodnja 'djen?	What day is it?
Воскресенье	Vaskri'senje	Sunday
Понедельник	Pani'djelnik	Monday
Вторник	'Ftornik	Tuesday
Среда	Sri'dah	Wednesday
Четверг	Chit'verk	Thursday
Пятница	'Pjahtnitsa	Friday
Суббота	Su'bota	Saturday
Рабочий (нерабочий) день	Ra'bochij (nira'bochij) 'djen.	Working (non-working) day
Неделя	Ni'delja	Week
Месяц	'Mjesits	Month
Год	Got	Year
Январь	Jin'var	January
Февраль	Fi'vrahlj	February
Март	'Mart	March
Апрель	Ap'relj	April
Май	Maj	May
Июнь	I'junj	June
Июль	I'julj	July
Август	'Ahvgust	August
Сентябрь	Sin'tjahbr	September
Октябрь	Ok'tjabr	October
Ноябрь	Na'jahbr	November
Декабрь	Di'kahbr	December
Зима	Zi'mah	Winter
Весна	Vis'nah	Spring
Лето	'Ljeta	Summer

A SHORT PHRASE-BOOK

Осень	'Osin	Autumn
Праздник	'Prahznik	Holiday
Новый год	'Novij 'got	New Year

TIME

Который час?	Ka'torij 'chahs?	What time is it?
Девять часов утра (вечера)	'Djevit chi'sof ut'ra ('vechira).	Nine a.m. (p.m.)
Половина десятого	Pala'veena di'sjahtava.	Nine-thirty
В семь часов	'Fsjem chi'sof.	At seven o'clock
В... часов... минут	V... chi'sof... mi'nut.	At ... hours ... minutes
Утро, утром	'Utra, 'utram	Morning, in the morning
Вечер, вечером	'Vecher, 'vecheram	Evening, in the evening
День, днем	Djen, dnjom	Afternoon, in the afternoon
Ночь, ночью	Noch, 'nochju	Night, at night
Секунда	Si'kunda	Second
Минута	Mi'nuta	Minute
Час	Chahs	Hour
Полчаса	'Polchi'sah	Half-hour
Сегодня	Si'vodnja	Today
Завтра	'Zahftra	Tomorrow
Вчера	Fchi'rah	Yesterday
Позавчера	Pazafchi'rah	The day before yesterday
Послезавтра	Posli'zahftra	The day after tomorrow
На прошлой (следующей) неделе	Na 'proshloj ('sljedushij) ni'djeli	Last (next) week
В будущем месяце (году)	V'budushim 'mjesitsi (ga'du)	Next month (year)

COUNTING

Сколько?	'Skolka	How much (many)?
Один	a'deen	one
Два	dvah	two
Три	tree	three
Четыре	chi'tiri	four
Пять	pjaht	five
Шесть	shest	six
Семь	'sjem	seven
Восемь	'vosim	eight
Девять	'djevit	nine
Десять	'djesit	ten
Одиннадцать	a'deenatsit	eleven
Двенадцать	dvi'nahtsit	twelve
Тринадцать	tri'nahtsit	thirteen
Четырнадцать	chi'tirnatsit	fourteen
Пятнадцать	pit'nahtsit	fifteen
Шестнадцать	shis'nahtsit	sixteen

Семнадцать	sim'nahtsit	seventeen
Восемнадцать	vasim'nahtsit	eighteen
Девятнадцать	divit'nahtsit	nineteen
Двадцать	'dvahtsit	twenty
Тридцать	'treetsit	thirty
Сорок	'sorak	forty
Пятьдесят	piddi'sjaht	fifty
Шестьдесят	shizdi'sjaht	sixty
Семьдесят	'sjemdisit	seventy
Восемьдесят	'vosimdisit	eighty
Девяносто	divi'nosta	ninety
Сто	sto	one hundred
Двести	'dvjesti	two hundred
Триста	'treesta	three hundred
Четыреста	chi'tirista	four hundred
Пятьсот	pit'sot	five hundred
Шестьсот	shis'sot	six hundred
Семьсот	sim'sot	seven hundred
Восемьсот	vasim'sot	eight hundred
Девятьсот	divit'sot	nine hundred
Тысяча	'tisicha	one thousand

MONEY, PRICES

1 копейка	ad'nah ka'pejka	1 kopeck
2 копейки	'dvje ka'pejki	2 kopecks
3 копейки	'tree ka'pejki	3 kopecks
5 копеек	'pjaht ka'pejik	5 kopecks
10 копеек	'desjit ka'pejik	10 kopecks
15 копеек	pit'nahtsit ka'pejik	15 kopecks
20 копеек	'dvahtsit ka'pejik	20 kopecks
1 рубль	a'deen 'rubl	1 ruble
3 рубля	'tree ru'bljah	3 rubles
5 рублей	'pjaht ru'blej	5 rubles
10 рублей	'djesit ru'blej	10 rubles
25 рублей	'dvahtsit 'pjaht ru'blej	25 rubles
50 рублей	piddi'sjaht ru'blej	50 rubles
100 рублей	'sto ru'blej	100 rubles
Сколько стоит?	'Skolka 'stojit?	How much does it cost?
Напишите, пожалуйста, цену.	Napi'shiti, pa'zhahlsta, 'tsenu.	Please write down the price
Сдача	'Zdahcha	Change

CHARACTERISTICS

| Хорош/-ий, -ая, -ее, -ие (masculine, feminine, neuter, plural) | Kha'rosh/-ij, -aya, -aje, -iji | Good |

Плох/-ой, -ая, -ое, -ие	Pla'kh/-oj, -aja, -oje, -eeji	Bad
Красив/-ый, -ая, -ое, -ые	Kra'seev/-ij, -aja, -aje, -iji	Pretty, beautiful
Некрасив/-ый, -ая, -ое, -ые	Nikra'seev/-ij, -aja, -aje, -iji	Ugly
Интересн/-ый, -ая, -ое, -ые	Inti-resn/-ij, -aja, -aje, -iji	Interesting
Неинтересн/-ый, -ая, -ое, -ые	Neinti'resn/-ij, -aja, -aje, -iji	Uninteresting
Дорог/-ой, -ая, -ое, -ие	Dara'g/-oj, -aja, -oje, -eeji	Expensive, dear
Дешев/-ый, -ая, -ое, -ые	Di'shov/-ij, -aja, -aje, -iji	Cheap
Быстр/-ый, -ая, -ое, -ые	'Bistr/-ij, -aja, -aje, -iji	Quick
Медленн/-ый, -ая, -ое, ые	'Mjedlin/-ij, -aja, -aje, -iji	Slow
Весел/-ый, -ая, -ое, -ые	Vi'sjol/-ij, -aja, -aje, -iji	Merry
Скучн/-ый, -ая, -ое, -ые	'Skushn/-ij, -aja, -aje, -iji	Dull

SIGNS

Внимание!	Vni'mahnije	Attention!
Стоп!	Stop	Stop!
Переход!	Piri'khot	Crossing
Остановка автобуса (троллейбуса, трамвая)	Asta'nofka af'tobusa (tra'lejbusa, tram'vaja)	Bus (trolley, tram) stop
Берегись автомобиля!	Biri'gees aftama'beelja!	Look out for cars!
Стоянка такси	Sta'jahnka tak'see	Taxi stand
Телефон-автомат	Tili'fon-afta'maht	Phone box
Справочное бюро	'Sprahvachnaje bju'ro	Information
Туалет (м) (ж)	Tua'ljet (mush'skoj, 'zhenskij)	Lavatory (Gents, Ladies)
Уборная (м) (ж)	U'bornaja (mush'skaja, zhenskaja)	Washroom (Gents, Ladies)
Аптека	Ap'tjeka	Chemist's
Почта. Телеграф	'Pochta. Tili'grahf	Post office, Telegraph office
Парикмахерская	Parik'mahkhirskaja	Beauty parlour, barber's shop
Театральная касса	Tia'trahlnaja 'kahssa	Box office (for a theatre)
Ресторан	Rista'rahn	Restaurant
Кафе	Ka'fe	Café
Булочная	'Bulashnaja	Bakery
Кондитерская	Kan'deetirskaja	Confectionery
Гастроном	Gastra'nom	Grocery (delicatessen)
Бакалея	Baka'leja	Grocery shop (flour, sugar, grains, etc.)
Мясо-рыба	'Mjahsa-'riba	Meat and fish
Закрыто	Za'krita	Closed
Открыто	At'krita	Open
Перерыв на обед	Piri'riv na a'bjet	Lunch break
Самообслуживание	'Sama-ap'sluzhivanje	Self-service
Вход (выход)	Fkhot/'vikhat	Entrance (exit)
Входа нет	'Fkhoda 'njet	No Entrance
Молоко	Mala'ko	Milk
Пиво-воды	'Peeva-'vodi	Beer/soft drinks
Соки-воды	'Soki-'vodi	Juices and mineral water

Вина, алкогольные напитки	'Veena	Wines, alcoholic drinks
Овощи-фрукты	'Ovashi-'frukti	Vegetables/fruit
Цветы	Tsvi'ti	Florist's
Парфюмерия	Parfju'mjerija	Perfumery
Табак (сигареты)	Ta'bahk, siga'reti	Tobacco
Книги	'Kneegi	Bookshop
Культтовары	Kultta'vari	Articles for cultural and recreational needs
Мебель	'Mjebil	Furniture store
Одежда	A'djezhda	Clothing store
Обувь	'Obuf	Shoe store
Головные уборы	Galav'nije u'bori	Hats
Галантерея	Galanti'reja	Haberdasher's
Детский мир	'Djetskij 'meer	Detsky Mir (children's goods)
Универмаг	Univir'mahk	Department store

THE METRO (M)

Вход	Fkhot	Entrance
Выход (выход в город)	'Vikhat ('vikhat v'gorat)	Exit (To the street)
Выхода нет	'Vikhada 'njet	No exit
Кассы	'kahssi	Ticket office
Опустите 5 копеек.	Apus'teeti 'pjaht ka'pejik	Drop 5 kopecks in the slot
Стойте справа, проходите слева.	'Stojti 'sprahva, prakha'deeti 'sljeva	Stand to the right, pass through on the left side
К поездам	K pajiz'dahm	To the trains
Пересадка на...	Piri'sahtka na...	Transfer to...

SHOPPING

Где ближайший магазин?	'Gdje bli'zhajshij maga'zeen?	Where is the nearest ... shop?
Покажите, пожалуйста.	Paka'zhiti, pa'zhahlsta.	I would like to see ... please
У вас есть...?	U'vahs 'jest...?	Do you have...?
Другого цвета	Dru'gova 'tsveta	Another colour
Другой фасон	Dru'goj fa'son	Another style
Больший (меньший) размер	'Bolshij ('mjenshij) raz'mjer	A larger (smaller) size
Я это куплю.	'Jah 'eta ku'plju.	I'll take that
Где я могу оплатить покупку?	'Gdje jah ma'gu apla'teet pa'kupku?	Where can I pay for this?

MEDICAL AID

Я нездоров (m) /нездорова (f).	'Jah nizda'rof/nizda'rova.	I am unwell

Я плохо себя чувствую.	'Jah 'plokha si'bja 'chustvuju.	I don't feel well
Вызовите, пожалуйста, врача.	'Vizaviti, pa'zhahlsta, vra'chah.	Please call a doctor
У меня температура.	U mi'njah timpira'tura.	I have fever
У меня болит голова (сердце, желудок, горло, глаз, рука, нога).	U mi'njah ba'leet gala'vah ('sjertse, zhi'ludak, 'gorla, 'glahs, ru'kah, na'gah).	My head (heart, stomach, throat, eye, hand, arm, leg) hurts/aches
Есть ли у Вас что-нибудь от простуды?	'Jest li u 'vahs 'shtonibut at pra'studi?	Do you have something for a cold?

EATING OUT

Дайте, пожалуйста, меню.	'Dajti, pa'zhahlsta, mi'nju.	Please bring me a menu
Принесите, пожалуйста, одну порцию (две порции)	Prini'seeti, pa'zhahlsta, ad'nu 'portsiju ('dvje 'portsiji).	Please bring me one serving (two servings) of ...
Принесите, пожалуйста, бутылку пива (вина, минеральной воды, коньяку, шампанского, водки).	Prini'seeti, pa'zhahlsta, bu'tilku 'peeva (vi'nah, mini'rahlnoj va'di, kanji'ku, sham'pahnskava, 'votki).	Please bring me a bottle of beer (wine, mineral water, cognac, champagne, vodka)
Стакан	Sta'kahn	Glass
Рюмка	'Rjumka	Wine-glass
Тарелка	Ta'rjelka	Plate
Нож	Nosh	Knife
Вилка	'Veelka	Fork
Ложка	'Loshka	Spoon
Салфетка	Sal'fjetka	Napkin
Скатерть	'Skahtirt	Tablecloth
Соль	Solj	Salt
Перец	'Pjerits	Pepper
Горчица	Gar'cheetsa	Mustard
Сахар	'Sahkhar	Sugar
Сливочное масло	'Sleevachnaje 'mahsla	Butter
Сигареты	Siga'reti	Cigarettes
Спички	'Speechki	Matches
Дайте, пожалуйста, счет.	'Dajti, pa'zhahlsta, 'shchot.	Please give me the bill

ON THE STREET

Скажите, пожалуйста, как пройти к гостинице...?	Ska'zhiti, pa'zhahlsta, 'kahk praj'tee ggas'teenitsi...?	Can you tell me how to get to the ... hotel?
Прямо, направо, налево, вперед, назад	'Prjahma, na'prahva, na'ljeva, fpi'rjot, na'zaht.	Straight ahead, to the right, to the left, ahead, back

Улица, площадь, переулок, перекресток, проспект, шоссе	'Ulitsa, 'ploshchit, piri'ulak, piri'krjostak, pras'pjekt, sha'se	Street, square, lane, cross-roads, prospekt, highway
Скажите, пожалуйста, Каким автобусом (троллейбусом, трамваем) я могу доехать до центра города (гостиницы..., ... вокзала)?	Ska'zhiti, pa'zhahlsta, ka'keem af'tobusam (tra'lejbusam, tram'vajam) 'jah ma'gu da'jekhat da'tsentra 'gorada (da ga'steenitsi..., da vag'zala)?	Can you tell me what bus (trolley, tram) I should take to get to the city centre (the ... Hotel, ... Railway Station)?
Покажите, пожалуйста, на карте, где я нахожусь.	Paka'zhiti, pa'zhahlsta, na'karti, 'gdje jah nakha'zhus.	Please show me on the map where I am
Я заблудился (*m*) /заблудилась (*f*)	'Jah zablu'deelsa /zablu'deelas.	I have lost my way
Милиционер	Militsia'njer	Militiaman
Как мне доехать до...?	'Kahk mnje da'jekhad da...?	How can I get (in a vehicle) to...?
Где пересадка на...?	'Gdje piri'sahtka na...?	Where is the transfer for...?
Сколько остановок до...?	'Skolka asta'novag da...?	How many stops to...?

DEPARTURE

Я уезжаю завтра в ... часов.	'Jah uji'zhaju 'zahftra v... chi'sof.	I am leaving tomorrow at ... o' clock
Приготовьте мне, пожалуйста, счет.	Priga'tofti 'mnje, pa'zhahlsta, 'shchot.	Please have my bill ready
Когда отходит поезд на...?	Ka'gdah at'khodit 'pojist na...?	When does the train for ... leave?
Где можно посмотреть расписание поездов (самолетов, пароходов)?	'Gdje 'mozhna pasma'tret raspi'sahnje pajiz'dof (sama'ljotaf, para'khodaf)?	Where can I look at a train (plane, boat) schedule?
Когда вылет самолета на... рейс...?	Kag'dah 'vilit sama'ljota na..., rejs...?	When does the flight ... for ... leave?
Вызовите, пожалуйста, такси.	'Vizaviti, pa'zhahlsta, tak'see.	Please call me a taxi
Где посадка на поезд номер... до...?	'Gdje pa'sahtka na'pojist 'nomir... da...?	Where do I board the train... for...?
Где посадка на самолет рейс номер... до...?	'Gdje pa'sahtka na sama'ljot 'rejs 'nomir... da...?	Where do I board flight No. ... for...?
С какой платформы отходит поезд номер... до...?	Ska'koj plat'formi at'khodit 'pojist 'nomir... da...?	What track does train No. ... for ... leave from?

MOSCOW IN TRANSIT

If you are travelling on business or for pleasure from Europe to the countries of East and South-East Asia and would like to visit Moscow, the capital of the Soviet Union, take up Aeroflot's offer and do so in the shortest and easiest way.

There are direct Aeroflot flights from Moscow to the capitals and major industrial centres of 69 countries.

FLY WITH THE LARGEST AIRLINE IN THE WORLD!

The magazine will tell you about:

the most interesting sights and tourist centres in the Soviet Union;
monuments of the history and culture of the peoples of the Soviet Union and their national customs
and arts;
museums and art galleries, theatres and sports;
Soviet economic and scientific achievements;
the amazing diversity of the country's natural beauty;
news about foreign tourism in the Soviet Union.

Travel to the USSR is an illustrated magazine appearing six times a year. It is read
in 60 countries in English, French, German and Russian, by all who are interested
in travel in the Soviet Union.
If you wish to visit the Soviet Union the magazine will tell you when and where
to go, what to see, and how to make your trip convenient and enjoyable.
Travel to the USSR will be your guide, friend and adviser during your stay
in the Soviet Union.

ИБ № 7254

Редактор русского текста *В. Остроумов*
Контрольный редактор *И. Ромашкевич*
Художник *М. Занегин*
Художественный редактор *В. Завадовская*
Технический редактор *В. Паленцева*

Сдано в набор 1. II. 1979 г.   Подписано в печать 24. X. 1979 г.
Формат 84 × 108/32   Бумага мелованная   Гарнитура Таймс
Печать офсетная   Условн. печ. л. 10,5   + печ. л. вклеек 1   Уч.-изд. л. 17,60
Тираж 140.000 экз.   Заказ № 005008/1   Цена 1 руб. 90 коп.   Изд. № 27440

Издательство «Прогресс» Государственного комитета СССР по делам
издательств, полиграфии и книжной торговли.
Москва, 119021, Зубовский бульвар, 17

Изготовлено в ГДР